EX LIBRIS

LETTERS FOR PILGRIMAGE:
LENTEN MEDITATIONS FOR TEEN GIRLS

Sarah Lenora Gingrich & A. N. Tallent

PARK END BOOKS

Sugar Land
2021

Letters for Pilgrimage: Lenten Meditations for Teen Girls
Copyright 2021 Sarah Lenora Gingrich and A. N. Tallent

All rights reserved. No part of this publication may be reproduced by any means, electronic, mechanical, photocopying, recording, scanning, or otherwise, without the prior written permission of the Publisher.

Published by:
    Park End Books
    5518 Linden Grove Ct
    Sugar Land, TX 77479

Cover art and chapter illustrations: Ned Bustard
Cover art copyright Ned Bustard, 2021.
Cover design: Summer Kinard

Publisher's Cataloging-in-Publication Data

Names: Gingrich, Sarah Lenora, 1980- author.
    Tallent, A. N., 1987- author.
Title: Letters for pilgrimage: Lenten meditations for teen girls / co-authored by Sarah Lenora Gingrich and A. N. Tallent; illustrations by Ned Bustard; designed by Summer Kinard
Description: Sugar Land [Texas]: Park End Books, 2021.
Identifiers:
ISBN: 978-1-953427-08-3
Subjects:
    Young Adult Nonfiction/Religious/Christian/Devotional & Prayer
    Young Adult Nonfiction/Religious/Christian/Inspirational

Library of Congress Control Number: 2021900527

Scripture taken from the New King James Version®. Copyright © 1982 by Thomas Nelson. Used by permission. All rights reserved.

www.ParkEndBooks.com

For our daughters, Sophia and Nicole, with love.

That very day two of them were going to a village named Emmaus, about seven miles from Jerusalem, and talking with each other about all these things that had happened. While they were talking and discussing together, Jesus himself drew near and went with them. So they drew near to the village to which they were going. He appeared to be going further, but they constrained him, saying, "Stay with us, for it is toward evening and the day is now far spent." So he went in to stay with them. When he was at table with them, he took the bread and blessed, and broke it, and gave it to them. And their eyes were opened and they recognized him; and he vanished out of their sight. They said to each other, "Did not our hearts burn within us while he talked to us on the road, while he opened to us the scriptures?"
-LUKE 24: 13-15, 28-29

Table of Contents

Introduction: Pack Your Bags	i
Week One: Leave-taking	1
Beginning our Journey	
Week Two: Thorns and Thickets	25
Trials and Temptations	
Week Three: Fellow Pilgrims	47
People and Stories to Light the Way	
Week Four: Methods of Travel	69
Spiritual Disciplines to Steady our Feet	
Week Five: Rest for the Weary	95
Comfort in the Midst of Hard Travel	
Week Six: Here There Be Dragons	117
When Our Journey is Treacherous	
Week Seven: Following the Master	141
Tracing Christ's Steps to the Cross	
Week Eight: Into the Kingdom	163
Basking in His Light	
References	187
About the Authors	188

Pilgrimage (noun):
a long journey to a sacred place to learn about God and about yourself as someone God loves

"Blessed is the one whose strength is in You,
Whose heart is set on pilgrimage."
Psalm 84:5

INTRODUCTION: PACK YOUR BAGS!

Almost 400 years after Christ walked the earth, a woman named Egeria went on a pilgrimage. She traveled extensively over the Mediterranean on the most epic quest anyone could ever undertake: she was seeking God. She traveled to ancient Israel, wandered through Jerusalem, cast her eyes upon Mt. Zion, then jumped on a ship to hunt after the Apostles and the holy churches they founded all over the Roman Empire. She detailed everything in a series of notes to her Christian "sisters" in the hopes that the beauty and Christ-given glory that she encountered could be theirs as well. You can even read some of those letters today, as she continues to guide and inspire people long after her journey was concluded. Following in her adventurous spirit, this little devotional was born; a collection of Lenten letters written by two different "travelers" to our Christian sisters, wherever and whoever you may be.

If you've picked up this book, no doubt you are readying yourself for an adventure. Perhaps that's not how you'd describe Lent. Over forty days of intense fasting, long church services, and hyper-focusing on one's shortcomings hardly sounds like an exciting time at first glance. But only at first glance. In her wisdom, the Church has given us this time to prepare for the Feast of Feasts: Pascha, the glorious Resurrection of Jesus. In order to fully comprehend the gravity of that amazing day, we must empty ourselves of all that distracts and infects our souls.

Lent helps us to do this, to prepare ourselves for Christ. It is absolutely a journey (and a long one, at that!) which we make each year toward the sacred Kingdom of God as an act of our devotion and commitment to the One who made and saved us. Lent is our holy pilgrimage done wherever we are at this moment, but together as one body, one entity. We're excited to walk it with you this year!

Don't be fooled though; we, the authors, are not experts. Both of us will quickly tell you that, despite our years, we are really still novices. Maybe we've walked this particular journey more often than you, but that means very little in light of eternity. We aren't here to scold you when you stumble and fall. We've done plenty of stumbling and falling ourselves (as some of our letters will reveal!), and we know that Lent (like life) is hard. We still have far to go and much to learn, but, as your older sisters in Christ, we want to give you a leg up on your journey and pass on the things we've discovered. We are strangers to you, yes, but we are very fond of you, and we hope that as you read these letters, you can feel that fondness and hear it in a voice that you love.

To help, we've decided not to sign the letters with our real names. They wouldn't mean much to you anyway. Instead, we wanted to leave you with what could be called a "wish" for you on your journey. When we first discussed this idea, both of us immediately chose "perseverance" as the attribute we most identify with. Indeed, for a long trip, you will need lots of perseverance if you hope to make it to your destination. Another word for perseverance is "steadfastness." It evokes the image of staying true and standing firm no matter the difficulties that lie ahead. We have found these words to ring true in our lives, helping us through the darkest of times. We have chosen to sign our letters as your friends, Perseverance and Steadfast, in the hopes that these qualities will lodge into your heart and hold you through the journey ahead.

This book will take you from Clean Monday through Thomas Sunday (the first Sunday after Pascha). It includes one brief letter and Scripture verse for each day and will focus on different aspects of the Eastern Orthodox Lenten season. Our hope is that it will help enrich your Lenten experience and bring peace, encouragement, and instruction to your soul as you grow into Christlikeness.

We see our Lenten pilgrimage as a more compact version of our true Pilgrimage: life. Our time on Earth is one long journey toward God (for some this is a joy, for others a horror). What we learn during this Lenten season, we hope to carry through our lives. We decided to write this book because Lent is too important to ignore or put off, and sometimes we need a little guidance (or a road map) to find our way through it.

You are in a beautiful and difficult period of your life. The things you learn and experience now will help to shape you into the woman you are just becoming. The two of us remember these years clearly and wish we had understood Lent then as we do now. We hope that we can pass on to you some of the gold and gems we've acquired on the way, while also equipping you with tools to defeat the monsters that we've had to face down.

Ideally, you would read one letter a day and meditate on the Scripture accompanying it, but we know things happen. You might forget one day or skip ahead a little. That's ok. No judgment. Do your best. Our letters will still be here whenever you get to them. But, please, do try to get to them! Each one was prayerfully written with you in mind. We don't want you to miss out on something that God may be trying to give to you through them.

Read the Scripture verse for each day several times out loud so that you can hold it in your heart and chew on it throughout your day. Each one is from a Psalm and links to one of our letters. If you have more time for prayer and study on some days, try reading that entire Psalm out loud. But, please know that these are only suggestions, not requirements. If you read one letter a day, that's perfectly fine. Do that, and be blessed.

You may be wondering why the art in this book doesn't look like other "girl" devotionals (no flowers or pastels, etc.). As we said before, Lent is an adventure, and the truth of it is, neither of us think the idea of quests and glory should be limited to just men. Many female saints lived lives that were full of adventure! Both of us tend to resist stereotyping, wanting instead to be true to our full personalities (a wild tree-hugger who knows martial arts, and a nerdy Goth who owns a sword). There's a time and place for flowers and pastels, but we feel that the Lenten season is a perilous quest, fit for the daring adventurer to traverse. We have trails to run, dragons to slay, forests to navigate, and the best of companions to share the load! Come, discover them all with us. Let's pack our bags and, with the Holy Spirit as our guide, step one foot out the front door and into the vast, exciting unknown.

Tying Our Shoes,
Steadfast and Perseverance

WEEK ONE: LEAVE-TAKING
BEGINNING OUR JOURNEY

WEEK ONE, DAY ONE
CLEAN MONDAY

"In You, O Lord, I put my trust;
Let me never be put to shame.
Deliver me in Your righteousness, and cause me to escape;
Incline Your ear to me, and save me.
Be my strong refuge,
To which I may resort continually;
You have given the commandment to save me,
For You are my rock and my fortress."
Psalm 71:1-3

Dear One,

There is a danger in pilgrimage, that in our planning and in our striving that we forget why we're making the journey, and to Whom. I have always loved to learn as part of my love of God, but I haven't always been great at focusing on the goal. I remember laying out my outfit, including which shoes I'd wear, and double-checking the supplies list, which hung limp in my hands from much refolding, highlighting, and being shoved in my pocket on trips to the store. The new school year loomed before me, and I didn't want to begin badly by forgetting the right kind of calculator or the specific kind of spiral bound, college-rule notebooks.

I couldn't help but make all sorts of promises and resolutions to myself that this year I was going to be super organized in my note taking. This year I wasn't going to put off homework until the last minute. This year I wasn't going to forget to study for tests and quizzes. I loaded my backpack up with my supplies and fervent hopes, a heavy load to shoulder. I got lost sometimes in my preparations for learning. I forgot that the goal of all my knowing was to know God.

Our Lenten journey may begin quite the same. This year I won't complain [much] about beans and hummus. This year I'll get organized and disciplined in my prayer life. This year I'll be kinder to my siblings and more helpful at home. This year I'll pay more attention during the services and not let my mind wander.

There is nothing wrong with our hopes; indeed, we probably need to grow into these aims. We miss something crucial though, if we focus on our personal goals rather than on Christ Himself. We miss what it is to be a pilgrim if we seek mainly to journey well, without thinking of Whom we are journeying to.

Pilgrimage is a journey undertaken to draw near to Christ, whether physically–traveling to holy sites, shrines, saints' relics–or spiritually–navigating the risks and rewards of the road in the heart and body. Just like physical travel, spiritual pilgrimages like that of Great Lent are not undertaken alone or without God's care and provision. We have fellow pilgrims, our fellow Christians and the saints, to help us; we have inns of rest to nourish us and strengthen us. And, too, there are dangers, dragons, and foes. We'll face them together with the tools that Christ has given us, with His saints alongside, beckoning us onward.

Your Fellow Pilgrim,
Perseverance

WEEK ONE, DAY TWO

"Show me Your ways, O Lord;
Teach me Your paths.
Lead me in Your truth and teach me,
For You are the God of my salvation;
On You I wait all the day."
Psalm 25: 4-5

Dear Adventurer,

My first airplane ride was also my first grand adventure: I was twelve, and my family was moving from my childhood home in Pennsylvania to tropical Florida, a strange land almost a thousand miles away and where we knew no one. I didn't want to go. My grandparents, cousins, best friends, school, and home were all here! Why would I want to go someplace where everything was unfamiliar and I would be a stranger? Flying didn't even excite me; I could only sob as I watched my beloved land disappear beneath me while that hunk of metal took me to places unknown.

Many years later I'd find myself on a bigger airplane and an even bigger adventure: I was going to Japan. Everything within me bubbled in excitement. I'd dreamed of this trip, longed to enter this foreign and completely different country, and now it was time! I wasn't dreading the journey or afraid of being in a place where I wouldn't know the language or customs. I was ready to explore, ready to see what Japan was all about. I couldn't wait to get on that jet!

Now, we have just begun the season of Lent. Which journey is it for you? Are you excited, eager to explore and discover what God has for you this year? Or is it difficult? Are you dreading these long days of fasting and extra church services, eager for it to be over so that you can enjoy spring and warmth and the food and time to yourself that you once enjoyed? Strangely enough, though I hated everything about Florida, I've made friends there that I've kept for life (including finding my husband!), and though Japan was beautiful and fun, the culture shock was hard, and sometimes I really missed home. The attitude we have towards Lent is important, but it doesn't mean we're doomed for a dreadful journey or guaranteed an easy one.

In *The Fellowship of the Ring*, we find Frodo beginning his journey with Samwise, who is fearful of taking the step that will bring him out of the Shire. They're later joined by Merry and Pippin, two frolicsome hobbits who find the idea of adventure exciting, eager to be on the road. Which hobbit are you feeling like today? Is Lent something you're jumping into or being dragged through? Hold those feelings loosely. The journey is long, and we cannot always see the path before us to the treasures and trials that await us. Ready yourself for trouble and hope for gold and jewels. Both are down this path.

Your Companion,
Steadfast

WEEK ONE, DAY THREE

*"Blessed is everyone who fears the Lord,
Who walks in His ways."*
Psalm 128:1

Dear Ascender of Heights,

I sat with my gear spread out on the ground in front of me, laid bare before the inspection of our guide. Sleeping bag, ground mat, basic toiletries, a few sets of clothing, a collapsible fishing pole, knife. He patiently set aside anything that wasn't absolutely necessary, and told us to repack. I remember thinking it a very strict affair; why would it matter if someone brought extra stuff they liked?

We were all young teen girls, embarking on a weeklong backpacking trip in the Montana wilderness. Feeling like top-heavy turtles, we took to the trail with joy and ease. After heading up the mountains for hours, the guide's counsel on acceptable pack weight suddenly made so much sense. Our leg muscles screamed, and our breath was labored. Any time we stopped to purify water from a crystal clear stream, our packs were shed with joy, everyone stretching like cats and feeling liberated.

Our guide had a lot of experience in what young legs could handle in rigorous ascent. His strictness was compassionate and wise. He knew that if we labored under too heavy a burden, we'd be vulnerable to giving up entirely, or injuring ourselves out of pride.

Lent seems a very strict time, does it not? There are many services to attend, many guidelines on what we can eat and when. It can all seem a bit much, can't it? When I scrambled up those mountains, bent low below my pack, sweating great rivulets down my face under the blazing, ever-so-near sun, I was glad to not be carrying even an ounce more, and gave thanks for the rule.

Rules are not lifegiving if we don't experience how they help us. The strictness of Great Lent is not a set of rules for the sake of rules, but a "rule of life," a discipline, a direction borne of wisdom that helps us towards our goals. St. Mark the Ascetic said, "Do not think about or do anything without a spiritual purpose, whereby it is done for God. For if you travel without purpose, you shall labor in vain."

The short-term changes in our daily life are given by our wise Guide, who knows the road we travel on, the trials we'll meet there, and how strong we must become to persevere. Try to keep that in your mind; you are being equipped for battle.

Pressing Onward, Upward,
Perseverance

WEEK ONE, DAY FOUR

"Search me, O God, and know my heart;
Try me, and know my anxieties;
And see if there is any wicked way in me,
And lead me in the way everlasting."
Psalm 139:23-24

Dear Beloved Daughter,

Before long road trips, I make sure everything is perfect: I make a list of all we'll need weeks in advance of the trip, we plan out our path and itinerary and reserve our campsite, I make sure all the clothes I'll need are washed, we find just the right snacks, the best music, and the car is given a full tank of gas. By the time we leave, we feel comforted by our preparations, certain that everything will work out as planned. When it doesn't–as is inevitable since we cannot foresee the future–I'm upset. This wasn't how it was supposed to go. It's not how I planned it.

I planned a lot in my life. I had goals and the drive to pursue them. I followed every prescribed path to get there, did everything right, and yet it was meaningless. I'm not using my college degree. I'm not living where I thought I would be. I'm a mother, and that was not something I thought I'd ever be. If you went back five years ago and told me what my life would be like now, I'd have laughed you out of the building. I had a plan. I was going to do it, and do it right.

However, God had better plans for me, and, one by one, He had to strip me of my goals and dreams until I finally surrendered to Him. And, you know what? His way is better: wilder, more uncertain, messier, but better. I'm happier now than I've ever been.

These plans, these goals, are my way of maintaining control. I have preconceptions of how things should be, and I do everything to keep them that way. The problem is, that leaves very little room for interruptions, even interruptions from God.

Our world pushes us to make five-year plans, life goals, and strategies for success. To deviate from these is seen as irresponsible. But God doesn't work that way. He doesn't give us a road map for our entire life's journey, but just enough direction for each day.

Sometimes, this makes me nervous. I want to see what's down the bend! I want to plan and prepare and be in control. But I am never truly in control, am I? It is God's world, after all, not mine.

There's nothing wrong with being prepared or having goals, but we need to hold them loosely, giving them back to God and joyfully accepting any deviations He gives.

He loves us. He made us. He's in control, and we are better for it.

As you're beginning this journey of Lent, do you have a plan? Are you aiming to fast strictly, attend as many church services as possible, read and pray twice as much as you do now? None of those things are bad in and of themselves, but if you are aiming for perfection, ask yourself why.

Is it because you want to be in control? What happens if you get sick and miss a service? Or if you visit a non-Orthodox friend who serves you ice cream? What if you miss your wake-up alarm and have no time to pray your usual prayers in front of the icons before you catch the bus? Will that frustrate you? Will you bemoan your circumstances or beat yourself up because of it?

Hold your plans loosely.

We do not know what God has in store for us on this journey, and if we try too hard to control it, to stick to the plan no matter what, we might miss the bigger and better lesson God has for us.

With Love,
Steadfast

WEEK ONE, DAY FIVE

*"I will praise You, for I am fearfully and wonderfully made;
Marvelous are Your works,
And that my soul knows very well."*
Psalm 139:14

Dear Enough,

It's strange what scenes imprint themselves on our memory. I was thirteen or so, sitting perched on the bathroom sink so that I could get very close to the toothpaste-splattered mirror. I observed the size of my pores, the pimples, the shape of my eyebrows, and the size of my bumpy nose from each angle. Nothing was to my satisfaction; all of it was wrong. I could not will it to change, and I despaired.

There was a pattern for the beautiful, and my incongruous features were not the pieces needed. I didn't look like my Barbies (not that I'd admit that I still secretly played with them). I didn't look like the models in the magazines, nor the actresses on tv. How would I live without beauty in a world that so highly prized it?

Well, I gave my unremarkable face a mask of sorts; heavy eyeliner, black mascara, and too often, a dark scowl as the final touch. If I couldn't be beautiful, I'd be fierce. It was indeed a mask; I was not brave, not fierce, just really sad to be so ordinary. I lived my life as a question mark: Am I enough? Am I accepted? Am I worthy? My mask was in place in case the answers were no.

I don't know exactly when it happened, but as I passed through the years I seemed to grow into my face, to claim it as mine, and to inhabit my imperfect body with comforting ease. I noticed also that beauty defied narrow patterns. It was there in the face of an older Philippine nun, her smile radiating 10,000 watts of joyful light. It was there in the tender look in my mother's eyes when she held her grandbabies. It was there in the network of wrinkles when my grandmother laughed. Beauty thrives in the flaws, as bees do in the wild, weedy ditches and thickets, finding the nectar that nature, left to its own devices, lifts up for them.

We travel our pilgrimages embodied; it is our bodies that kneel, lay prostrate, that lift our arms to cross ourselves, that bend our backs to venerate. It is quite normal to not feel at home in your body, to not fully embrace the texture of our hair, the features of our faces, the need for a wheelchair or thick glasses, the generous curves or the lack thereof. But as an older sister, (and here I hope you can feel my spontaneous hug) I assure you that so very much beauty, so much light and grace, are hidden in your "flaws". God knows how to shape us; can we trust His wisdom? Can we hold out hope that beauty thrives in the imperfect? Our bodies are needed to make this journey; we must make friends with them.

Happy Now With The Same Bumpy Nose,
Perseverance

WEEK ONE, DAY SIX

*"And let the beauty of the Lord our God be upon us,
And establish the work of our hands for us;
Yes, establish the work of our hands."*
Psalm 90:17

Dear Hero-In-Training,

My grandmother is a world-class traveler. She's been to Europe, Israel, Canada, and almost every US state. It wasn't uncommon for her and my grandfather to disappear for an entire summer as they road-tripped across the country. During one of these adventures, I received a call from her. They were traveling out West, and my grandmother was thoroughly bored.

"We're in Kansas," she told me, laughing. "And there's nothing in Kansas!" She had merely called me to help pass the time looking at endless cornfields.

I read a lot of books about heroes and adventurers or biographies of famous and extraordinary people. They all seem to have such exciting, fast-paced lives. But, read between the lines of these tales: the large events or heroic deeds are only part of their stories. It only takes up maybe one year or one week or one day of their life!

In between is monotony, the day-to-day routine, the same old, same old. Abraham Lincoln had years of ordinary life and work before he became president. Harry Potter had school classes and homework in between fights with the Dark Lord. The Pevensie children were having a dreary, boring afternoon indoors when Lucy found the wardrobe that led her to Narnia. We tend to focus on the large, amazing events of both history and fiction, but surrounding all these accomplishments and noble quests are the tedious, ho-hums of the everyday, the cornfields in Kansas.

Right now, we're still in the first week of Lent. Things are still exciting and new, the foods still exotic, the services still fresh. But that's quickly going to change. In just a few days, the soup that you enjoyed will become, "Ugh, lentils again?". Those prostrations will become annoying. The long prayers will make you want to doze. Monotony is going to set in.

The funny thing about these boring days is that they are necessary to our spiritual development. If we want to accomplish great things and see the face of God, our training ground starts in these unexciting days and weeks ahead.

Abraham Lincoln's diligence in school and work helped prepare him to become a great president. Harry Potter's days in monotony gave him an appreciation for the life he had and the resilience to fight the evil that threatened it. If Peter, Edmund, Susan, and Lucy hadn't been stuck inside on a rainy day, they would have never reigned as kings and queens in Narnia.

God is preparing us for bigger things, for Himself. We don't just wake up one day and become heroes. That transformation takes place day by day, bit by bit, as we take on the small challenges of every day.

If you can develop patience while enduring the trials of Lent, you'll have it when true and sudden hardship comes your way. If you can train yourself to focus on God during these long services, you'll see Him when terrible temptations and griefs threaten to overwhelm you.

If you can learn now to stand up to the sin in your own heart, you'll be better prepared to stand up for what's right in the world around you.

Don't begrudge the cornfields of Kansas. They are helping you become who God made you to be.

Cheering You On,

Steadfast

WEEK ONE, DAY SEVEN
SUNDAY OF ORTHODOXY

"Preserve me, O God, for in You I put my trust.
O my soul, you have said to the Lord,
'You are my Lord,
My goodness is nothing apart from You.
As for the saints who are on the earth,
They are the excellent ones, in whom is all my delight."
Psalm 16:1-3

Dear Traveler,

We come to the first Sunday of Great Lent, The Triumph of Orthodoxy, which celebrates the return of the icons to the churches and the defeat of the iconoclastic heresy. The Kontakion proclaims:

"No one could describe the Word of the Father;
But when He took flesh from you, O Theotokos, He accepted to be described,
And restored the fallen image to its former beauty.
We confess and proclaim our salvation in word and images."

At my prayer corner I raise my eyes to the icons of Christ, the Theotokos, and beloved saints. In each of their images I find myself being confronted by their lives. How they lived left footprints along the Way, and their images remind me where I too must walk. Our world is full of imagery; the famous, the rich, the powerful are plastered everywhere, each expressing a worldly vision of success. When I look at the icons of the saints, I see an altogether different definition of greatness: dying to self, humility, love, kindness, bravery, purity, selflessness.

As we journey along, we'll be reminded that the saints are not just part of the Church's past, but are actively at work here in the present. They are always praying for us, and their icons remind us of their unseen presence. Their stories teach us how to respond faithfully and bravely to the challenges, trials, and temptations that threaten to strike us aside, down, and away from our destination.

If you've ever traveled internationally, you'll know the profound relief of being helped by someone who can translate for you when your attempts at communication have failed, or helped you to find your hotel, or a bathroom. The saints are familiar with the road we must travel, well-versed in the hazards we'll face and the tools we'll need to keep our feet on the trail. Glory to God that we have their stories and their prayers as guides as we walk; may we glorify Him as they did on earth and now do in Heaven.

With You,
Perseverance

WEEK TWO: THORNS AND THICKETS
TRIALS AND TEMPTATIONS

WEEK TWO, DAY ONE

> "Listen, O daughter,
> Consider and incline your ear;
> Forget your own people also, and your father's house;
> So the King will greatly desire your beauty;
> Because He is your Lord, worship Him."
> Psalm 45:10-11

Dear Woman of God,

As we round the bend and enter into the second week of Lent, home has faded into the distance and our journey has taken a new shape. Now the novelty is wearing off and all around us are dark paths, tall trees, silence, and the unknown. It is here that we begin to trip over stones and have the potential for losing our way as trials and temptations litter our path and attempt to steer us off course. During this week, we'll explore some of these trials and temptations that follow us in life, berating us, annoying us, and tricking us into turning away from God.

As women, we are subject to unique trials and temptations. Our society has very narrow definitions of how we should behave, dress, think, work, and speak, and these definitions change as you go from one social sphere to the next. A woman must conform to certain standards of beauty. Or perhaps she should always be nice, never contradicting what anyone else says. A woman should be powerful. She should like only certain activities. A woman should stay in the home. Or perhaps a woman should stay in the business world and forgo having a family. A good woman gets married. A good woman doesn't need a man. A woman is a servant of hospitality. No, a woman is a queen. The messages are endless and the pressure is real. If we step one toe out of line, we are told that somehow we are a disgrace to our gender, but what that means changes from place to place and year to year. When you are young and trying to find your spot in the world, these contradicting messages only add to your confusion and anxiety. And, of course, there is the temptation that if we don't "fit" into whatever definition of "woman" our society has in mind, that we must not be a woman at all, that God has somehow made a mistake in creating us.

Take a moment and shut out all of these screaming voices for a bit. You are made in the image of God. As far as you are following God and becoming more like Him, you are a true woman. Growth in Christ-likeness doesn't turn us into something else but makes us into who we truly are. God has made you -and me- as women and calls us to follow Him. That is true womanhood, no matter if we get married or stay single, have a career or children, wear makeup or not, enjoy traditional "feminine" activities or "masculine" hobbies, are quiet or outspoken. If you are following Christ with all your heart, soul, and mind, you are becoming a good woman no matter what our fallen society may say about you.

As you walk this path of Lent, try to focus on growth in Christ and ignore the tidal wave of messages that the world sends to us women. You will find authentic womanhood as you listen to His voice. The rest is just noise.

Truly Yours and God's,
Steadfast

WEEK TWO, DAY TWO

> *"Look upon me and be merciful to me,*
> *As Your custom is toward those who love Your name.*
> *Direct my steps by Your word,*
> *And let no iniquity have dominion over me.*
> *Redeem me from the oppression of man,*
> *That I may keep Your precepts.*
> *Make Your face shine upon Your servant,*
> *And teach me Your statutes."*
> Psalm 119:132-135

Dear Truest Sister,

I begged my parents for a jacket that I didn't even like, and particular black sneakers because they were "in". I needed (so I thought) the outward pieces of image and brand that would make me blend into my friend group seamlessly. I shoplifted, though terrified and ridden with guilt, because that was the thrill du jour for my peers. I was making decisions about my attire, my language, and my actions to fit a mold which was not me, not at all.

    I was unmoored from myself, because in reality I wanted to be wearing flowing dresses, hippie sandals, reading poetry rather than swearing like a pirate, and running through the woods, rather than the local mall. I was not strong enough then to be authentically me, if I could even have articulated who that was.

I gave my heart to Christ in a burst of repentance in the woods; I wanted the light that I saw in others to make its home within me. I wanted to be honestly whole, not this shell of peer expectations and fear. As I bumbled through learning to live out my faith, I could no longer maintain my collapsing facade; real me was emerging. I actually didn't want to swear every other word. I actually didn't want to try out drugs and alcohol as my friends were beginning to do. I actually wanted to invite beauty, poetry, art, history, science, and nature back into the main quarters of my heart and mind. My peers were walking in ways I could no longer walk in, and painfully, we parted ways.

When I first came to faith in Christ, my brother goaded me endlessly. His teasing grew so unbearable that one day I blew up at him in an awful outburst, which revealed much more about my pride than it did about his pestering. I had grown, but so had my ego, which undid everything. Oh, that I could spare others from making the same mistakes!

Whenever we try to live a more holy life, we will experience friction, even among Christian friends and family! There is a reason that the phrase "holier than thou" is always said with a sneer. We feel it too, when others surpass us spiritually, we may feel both convicted by their life and jealous, which can lead us into resentment, anger, and mockery. Some will reject changes in us, others may be intrigued, but regardless, we must keep our feet on the trail. Let us be humble pilgrims, bearing our burdens, with our eyes fixed on Him.

Ever-humbled,
Perseverance

WEEK TWO, DAY THREE

> *"Behold, You desire truth in the inward parts,*
> *And in the hidden part You will make me to know wisdom.*
> *Purge me with hyssop, and I shall be clean;*
> *Wash me, and I shall be whiter than snow."*
> Psalm 51:6-7

Dear Precious Pathfinder,

I was a freshman in college when I was unexpectedly summoned into the Dean's office. Waiting inside with him was the school chaplain and a close friend of mine. I had confided in this friend just a few nights ago about something I was involved in; something that in hindsight was very wrong and harmful. Unbeknownst to me, she was concerned for my soul (rightfully so) and had reported me to the Dean. This meeting was a confrontation. As I listened to the Dean ask me about what my friend had told him, I felt my cheeks flush with shame. Why would she tell on me?! Was I going to be in trouble? Would they kick me out? I couldn't bear to have my deeds exposed like this. So, I did the worst thing I could have possibly done in that situation: I lied.

I still wish I could erase that entire moment, how I threw my friend under the bus, told them she was mistaken, that I had no idea what she was talking about, how she must have misinterpreted what I said. I hate to admit this, but I'm a great liar. They believed me, and then I immediately ran off to discard all the evidence in my possession that proved what my friend said was actually true. The only silver lining is that I was scared enough by this encounter to fully abandon the sin I was entrenched in, but I also lost my friend in the process. We stopped talking to each other after that day, and she transferred to a different school the next semester. I often wonder if I was the reason she left.

Shame is such a devious temptation, a flashing warning sign on our path begging us to turn the wrong way because the road ahead looks scary. Shame promises safety if we hide and never come out, but the result is that it takes us in the complete opposite direction from where we want to go. I had a choice during that confrontation. What if I had swallowed my shame and admitted the truth? I was a very troubled student. Would they have gotten me help? Would I have saved my friendship instead of my pride? I'll never know. I was too afraid to do the right thing, so I heaped sin on top of sin, losing sight of my path toward Christ.

It would be many years before the Holy Spirit would convict me to finally stop lying. With much fear, I called my two best friends and confessed to the lies I had been telling them, including about the incident above. They were far more gracious than I deserved, and I was forgiven. My friendships were saved and my conscience was clear. Oh, I wish I'd had that bravery earlier in the Dean's office when my friend, with tears in her eyes, looked at me and said that she loved me! That love was why she had disclosed my evil secrets, and I rewarded her with selfishness and pain. Lord, have mercy on me, a sinner.

Staying True,
Steadfast

WEEK TWO, DAY FOUR

> *"Come, you children, listen to me;*
> *I will teach you the fear of the Lord.*
> *Who is the man who desires life,*
> *And loves many days, that he may see good?*
> *Keep your tongue from evil,*
> *And your lips from speaking deceit.*
> *Depart from evil and do good;*
> *Seek peace and pursue it."*
> Psalm 34:11-14

Dear Forthright,

Soon after we were married, we moved to Canada so my husband could complete his degree in Biblical Studies. We didn't have much money, and were regularly benefitting from a local farmer's free pile of potatoes and turnips in a root cellar on campus. As our savings dwindled, I sought work to help make ends meet.

    Word of mouth found me a job opening nannying two young boys. I interviewed and they were eager to hire me with one condition: it had to be under the table. They needed someone immediately, and couldn't wait for me to apply for a green card, which can take months. Though friends chided me, my conscience wouldn't allow me to accept the position illegally, no matter how very much I was growing tired of turnip soup and baked potatoes.

I did however decide to begin the process of getting a green card, so I'd be ready for any work I might find. Part of the process is getting a medical exam. The doctor sat me down at the end and gravely told me blood was found in my urine, and that one, or both, of my kidneys was infected. I'd had no symptoms; I'd felt perfectly well. He put me immediately on antibiotics which stopped the infection and saved my kidneys.

I often wonder what would have happened to me had I ignored the Holy Spirit's warning. What seemed like a needed gain could have turned into a major, irreversible loss. If you've ever learned orientation (using a compass and map to arrive at a particular destination) in school you know that a mistake in navigation doesn't seem like much in the beginning (you are perhaps a foot or two off the mark), but the inaccuracy magnifies the further you proceed, which can be hundreds of yards off target. Sins that seem small (only the Lord knows their true measure) have the same effect; they point us completely off from where we ought to be headed. In that veering course we no longer find ourselves slightly off track, but even gravely so, sometimes even lost.

Practical, useful, seemingly benign sins are darts that pierce the gaps of our armor. Let us be vigilant; let us give heed to the disquiet within us when we are tempted to do wrong. God will enable us to live with integrity, and He will provide, even if it means abundant turnip soup.

With Two Kidneys and Much Gratitude,
Perseverance

WEEK TWO, DAY FIVE

*"Through Your precepts I get understanding;
Therefore I hate every false way."*
Psalm 119:104

Dear Beautiful Heart,

Most years, my family would all pile into our plum minivan and drive from Florida up to Pennsylvania to visit our relatives. It was a very long trip, and to pass the time, we made up a game counting South of the Border billboards. These were huge, bright yellow, incredibly flashy signs spread over hundreds of miles with one goal in mind: trying to convince you to turn off the road and stay at the massive tourist attraction that lay just beneath the border of North and South Carolina. Indeed, when we would finally pass that location after counting two or three states worth of signs, it did look impressive! Flashing lights, a tall tower with a sombrero on top, it looked fun!

You are probably already aware of the huge, flashing billboards that litter our journey toward God. Our world has many opinions on where we should be headed. Signs, both literal and figurative, urge us to seek after beauty and follow the road of fashion, or insist that success is where we must be headed, following a path of perfection. Still louder, we're told that relationships and love are the most worthy goals of our lives, and sex and moral compromise can get us there the fastest. And if you think these signs are obnoxious now, just wait until you're a full-fledged adult. They're even louder, bigger, and harder to ignore.

Please don't misunderstand me: there is nothing wrong with caring for your appearance, wanting to do your best, or hoping to fall in love, but these things are not our destination, as nice as they are. Our journey's goal is to draw closer to God and become more like Him. These things can help us on our path, but they can also easily distract us into turning off the road and making them the object of our lives instead of Christ. I've seen the outcome of some of these paths: women who trade their health to look skinny and nearly die in the process, career workers who push and trample others in order to be the best, hasty relationships that become abusive or fall apart after a few years, leaving the couple broken. Check your heart and your focus. Are beauty, success, and romance nice side perks or things to be obtained at all cost? Have they become idols, replacing Christ on the altar of your heart? Is it time to turn around and get back on the right path?

On one trip, we finally did manage to persuade my parents to stop at South of the Border for the night. It wasn't at all what I expected. The rooms were small and cockroach laden, the place was noisy, and all the attractions were horribly overpriced. In the end, despite the flashy signs, it wasn't worth it. We let the signs tell us where we wanted to be, and they were wrong.

Staying the Course,
Steadfast

WEEK TWO, DAY SIX

"Let the words of my mouth and the meditation of my heart
Be acceptable in Your sight,
O Lord, my strength and my Redeemer."
Psalm 19:14

Dear Friend,

No matter how smoothly I spoke in Spanish, no matter how close my accent came to the lilting, melodic cadence of the southern Chilean accent, I was charged more for fruits, fish, and vegetables at the open-air market. My fair skin, light hair, and blue eyes marked me in their eyes as rich, foreign, American, in a word, "other." It didn't matter that I wasn't rich really, and that I very much had a grocery budget; the perception, the judgment was immovable, even with those I knew for years.

    I too have judged unjustly, far too many times to count. When I first had faith in Christ, I could so easily assess the lack of devotion in other believers. Why were they not full of joy like me? Why did they not study the Bible like me? Why weren't they eager to share the good news of Christ with others? I had so much to learn about who they actually were and who I was actually not. My zeal was infected with pride, rendering it noisy and useless. Oh, how God has humbled this bumbling Christian!

What is it like to be a humble person, one who sees her own vices and believes the best about her fellow pilgrims? Abba Dorotheos of Gaza shares a story of such a one:

> I heard about a certain brother who, if he saw that his cell was uncared for and disorderly when he went to consult any of the brethren, used to say to himself, 'Happy indeed is this brother! How free from care about many things, or rather, about all earthly things, and he so fixes his whole mind on high so that he has no leisure to put his cell in order.' And again, if he came on another and saw his cell in good order, clean, beautiful, he used to say to himself, 'The soul of this brother must be as clean and well-kept as his cell, for the good state of his soul must be represented by the good state of his cell.' He never said about anyone, 'This man is uncouth or that one is vainglorious', but on account of his own habitual good disposition he took edification from each of them.

I love the image of this humble monk who looks for the virtues rather than the failings of others. Imagine being so aware of our own sins, that we judge no one. In every situation he looked for the goodness of others and found an exhortation for himself. The enemy always wants us measuring others and not ourselves, because he knows that is where we'll begin to make real progress.

Knowing that the journey towards Christ is arduous and full of peril, we must keep our eyes on our own steps, not on those of others. Have you ever laughed at someone slipping on ice, and then you yourself fell? Have you called someone a gossip behind their back, and then had the reality of your hypocrisy bloom in your heart? The surest way to fall is to eagerly watch for others to do so.

In Christ,
Perseverance

WEEK TWO, DAY SEVEN
SUNDAY OF ST. GREGORY PALAMAS

"O God, You are my God;
Early will I seek You;
My soul thirsts for You;
My flesh longs for You
In a dry and thirsty land
Where there is no water.
So I have looked for You in the sanctuary,
To see Your power and Your glory."
Psalm 63:1-2

Dear Seeker of God,

In the early 1300s, a scholar named Barlaam taught that all one needed in order to know God was a rational mind. One should only seek education and knowledge in order to try to understand God. After all, God cannot be truly known, so Barlaam taught, and therefore all we can do is cling to concepts and philosophies about Him. The idea of hearing from God in prayer or experiencing Him physically was nothing but nonsense.

These ideas sound very familiar, don't they? Our current scientific society says much the same. Knowledge is the "end all". The rational brain is what makes us human. God is far beyond us. Miracles don't exist. This is a tempting philosophy to follow, and many, even God-fearing Christians, tread its path blindly. To insist otherwise is to be looked at as crazy, overly mystical, and "ignorant".

Today we celebrate the saint who heard Barlaam's arguments and refuted them. St. Gregory Palamas was a monk who insisted that God could be experienced and that we are not simply the sum of our minds. God's true Self, or "essence" may be beyond our reach, but His "energies" or direct actions could actually be discerned and felt by us mortals! Contemplative prayer and spiritual disciplines often give way for people to experience God in a real and direct manner. After all, God didn't only create brains. He made us with minds and bodies. Our entire being can experience Him whether it's through activities of the mind such as studying or through the body such as partaking in the Eucharist. Some monks, St. Gregory said, had even seen God's "uncreated light" as they prayed. That light is the Light which shone around Jesus during His

Transfiguration, a light which many saints have seen to this day.

Barlaam's perspective is, perhaps, one of the greatest temptations on our current journey. Our culture is so obsessed with the intellectual that the body is almost an afterthought, a means to an end. The miraculous is often written off as a hoax, and God is portrayed as a cold Mind who never reaches out to touch us. Resist the thorns and brambles that try to hold you to this path. God, in His energies, can be known, and the trials of Lent are meant to help us to do just that. Don't lose sight of our destination! It is God Himself, not merely a definition of Him.

Seeking With You,
Steadfast

WEEK THREE: FELLOW PILGRIMS

PEOPLE AND STORIES TO LIGHT THE WAY

WEEK THREE, DAY ONE

> *"Blessed are the undefiled in the way,*
> *Who walk in the law of the Lord!*
> *Blessed are those who keep His testimonies,*
> *Who seek Him with the whole heart!"*
> Psalm 119:1-2

Dear Servant of Christ,

It would happen to me every summer; I'd go off to Christian camp, get completely zealous about my faith, supercharged to live my life completely for Him, and then...I'd get home. The sparkles of transcendency fell to the floor I was asked to sweep, and my lofty exaltation ground down into the more sustainable level of daily struggle. I found my forsworn bad attitude showing up again, talking back to my parents, lying, leaving my room a mess. I fell as high as I'd thought I'd climbed. I should have come home to serve, not preach, to walk humbly, not put on spiritual airs, to struggle, not expect to float effortlessly through life on a spiritual high.

    I watched Nancy as she did the dishes. Everything about her spoke of an ongoing dialogue between her and

Christ, and if you watched her lips closely, you'd see them slightly mouth the prayers that were flowing silently from her heart. I learned more about being a Christian from watching my fellow missionary do the dishes than I ever did in my theological studies.

She didn't rush; she was deliberate, as though the glass she was rinsing would be set before Christ. She was careful with the water, using just enough, not wanting to waste the blessing of it down the drain. She struggled, as we all do, but it came from a fortified place within her where Christ held sway.

If you have such a holy person near you, by all means, pay attention. They are showing you things of the utmost importance: how to take up your cross, how to die to yourself, how to pray without ceasing, how to live and breathe Christ. Holy people may not be obvious; indeed, they are often humble and prefer to go unnoticed, but you can find them cleaning the kitchen with joy after coffee hour or holding an unhappy baby so its mother can have a break. Look for them, study them.

In this week's meditations we'll delve into the helpers, both fellow pilgrims and supernatural ones, who aid us to keep Christ-bound, our feet on the trail to life. It has been my experience that every time I asked God to help me, He sent someone to show me the way. He cares for His traveling children, and never, for even a moment, does He suffer us to travel truly alone.

Bumbling Forward,
Perseverance

WEEK THREE, DAY TWO

*"For He shall give His angels charge over you,
To keep you in all your ways."*
Psalm 91:11

Dearly Loved Soul,

I had just returned from a trip when it hit: the worst stomach flu of my life. I ran a high fever and vomited until there was nothing left in me to puke out. I couldn't keep down any food or drink, and, to make matters even worse, I was also on my period. In an instant, all my body's energy resources were gone until I lacked the strength to even move, lying on the bathroom floor next to the toilet in case I needed to hurl again. I lay there for three days. My parents told me they lacked the strength to carry me to my bed, and so they simply placed water by my face and tried to cover me with blankets and give me medicine. I was barely conscious of anything going on around me.

Suddenly, on the fourth day, I was aware of a presence next to me. I saw a friend of mine, and he leaned over and threw my arm around his neck. "Come on," he said. "We need to get you in bed." I distinctly recall him hoisting me up, letting me lean on him for support as he dragged me to my room and laid me in my bed. I didn't have the strength to move, but he had plenty for us both.

The next day, I was feeling so much better from not sleeping on a hard floor and was finally able to keep down some liquids. My parents were thrilled, since they had already decided that if I hadn't gotten up off the floor when I had, they'd have to call an ambulance and get me to a hospital. They weren't aware of any boy coming to help me, yet I distinctly remembered leaning on someone for support. To this day, I think it was my guardian angel in disguise, caring for me in ways no one else could, using his supernatural strength to lift me off the floor.

Mother Alexandra, in her book *The Holy Angels*, writes in great length about the angels God has sent to protect us. In fact, she even writes about a similar experience to mine, waking up one morning to see a group of angels huddled around her and her baby brother as they slept. The Church teaches us that we each have an angel assigned to aid us, though we may never see or touch them. Mother Alexandra explains that these angels don't look like what you see in decorations nowadays; they aren't cute, chubby kids with harps, but powerful beings of energy, often showing up as warriors and agents of light.

They constantly reflect God's attributes toward us, and our particular guardian is always at work guiding and encouraging the best of us, the parts made in God's image, to shine forth. Our sin can hinder them, but repentance brings them near again. Be comforted: on this journey they will ever accompany you. Mother Alexandra even suggests that they will be the ones to lift your soul to God, accompanying you even through death.

Sometimes, if I'm very still, I can almost feel my guardian's nudge, a gentle suggestion or reminder to do the right thing, hold my tongue, or be at peace. If I'm attentive, I can almost sense them singing alongside me at church, praising God in unfettered joy. Such a one is near you now as well. Take a breath. Be still. Can you almost hear them whisper?

Resting in Him,
Steadfast

WEEK THREE, DAY THREE

*"As for me, I will see Your face in righteousness;
I shall be satisfied when I awake in Your likeness."*
Psalm 17:15

Dear Pilgrim,

Some of us learn best by observing others first. As a child I'd sit across the kitchen counter from my mother as she'd knead bread dough and shape it carefully into rolls. Seeing her work informed my hands on how to stretch, push, and tuck the dough, long before I was ready to make my own bread. Watching an older friend of mine responding with grace and prayer to unexpected circumstances informed my heart on how to steady the inner boat when the waves inevitably crash. Slow down, breathe. I had these living patterns to follow; I didn't have to figure everything out on my own, but could access embodied skills and virtues I'd witnessed.

To read about a saint is to fall in love. Whether my own wild saint, St. Mary of Egypt, or revered St. Basil, or a holy fool like St. Xenia, there is a warmth in our hearts when we read their stories; we are learning how God heals and makes holy all sorts of humans, with all sorts of spiritual maladies. We get to see how they lived the faith, learned to pray, wrestled with sin and temptation, and grew.

But they are not just static history either, but active participants in our journeys. They pray for us, and sometimes they even appear in visions or dreams...

I dreamt that I was in a church, milling around after a service, when St. Paisios of Mount Athos walked in with a determined stride. I marveled, "What? I thought he was dead!" He walked up to me, reached to cup my head between his hands and brought his forehead against my own, giving me a bonk. He then reprimanded me for something which I cannot recall, and briskly ended with "I like your husband." Off he strode and the vision ended. He was a saint on a mission! Places to be, people to bonk! It may seem silly; it definitely seemed odd to me, until I read later about how he'd "disguise" blessing others by playfully bonking them on the head! I awoke, pouting, "But what about me? Do you like me?" Needless to say, my husband chose St. Paisios as his saint, or was it the other way around?

The saints are here for us; they are ready to help us journey towards Christ. They are travelers with experience, and we can carry within our hearts their examples of how to die to self and live to Christ. They are only a prayer away.

In His Care,
Perseverance

WEEK THREE, DAY FOUR

"Let the proud be ashamed,
For they treated me wrongfully with falsehood;
But I will meditate on Your precepts.
Let those who fear You turn to me,
Those who know Your testimonies."
Psalm 119:78-79

Dear Friend of the Road,

The Old Testament tells us that, after King Solomon died, his son, Rehoboam, was crowned king. II Chronicles 10 details how all the people of Israel came to Rehoboam and asked him to "lighten their load" and relieve them of the heavy work and taxes his father had imposed upon them. The new king then decided to ask for advice from two different sets of people. One was a group of elders who had served his father. They advised him to give in to the people's wishes and thus earn their respect and loyalty. The second group was Rehoboam's childhood friends. Listen to the advice they give him:

"Then the young men who had grown up with him spoke to him, saying, "Thus you should speak to the people who have spoken to you, saying, 'Your father made our yoke heavy, but you make it lighter on us'—thus you shall say to them: 'My little finger shall be thicker than my father's waist! And now, whereas my father put a heavy yoke on you, I will add to your yoke; my father chastised you with whips, but I will chastise you with scourges!'"

–II Chronicles 10:9-11

This is the prideful advice that the young king took, and the result was disastrous: the people rebelled and the kingdom of Israel split in two with the northern kingdom fighting the south for generations. The strength of the great nation of God was divided and would eventually be conquered by Babylon and Assyria, all because of advice that stroked the king's pride instead of urging him to be humble.

Think of your own life and your own circle of friends, the people accompanying you on this journey of Lent. When difficulties confront you, do they encourage you to act in humility and grace? Or do they stir up your anger and pride, wanting to see you lash out? Do your friends respect your journey towards God? Or do they put down your faith and feelings, wanting you to act in your (or their) own interests instead of that of God and others?

Sometimes it's as simple as noting how you feel around someone: do you leave their presence with an abundance of peace and gratitude, or do you feel stirred up, anxious, angry, or belittled? Those latter emotions can be a good sign that perhaps there is someone in your life who is bringing out the worst in you, and it might be time to close your ears to their advice and seek companionship elsewhere.

As we see in Rehoboam, the people we choose to travel with on this journey make a huge impact on our lives. They can help us on our path to God or they can pull us onto a different path that ultimately leads to pain and destruction. Take this time to make a list of the friends closest to you and prayerfully ask God to reveal to you which type they are. Don't be afraid to ask advice from your parents, godparents, or parish priest! Sometimes it takes an outsider's perspective to help us see what's going on within us and our circle of friends.

Your Friend Forever,
Steadfast

WEEK THREE, DAY FIVE

> *"Let the righteous strike me;*
> *It shall be a kindness.*
> *And let him rebuke me;*
> *It shall be as excellent oil;*
> *Let my head not refuse it."*
> Psalm 141:5

Dear Sojourner,

It is startling how very accompanied we are at all times. Our guardian angels are ever near. God sees and hears us. Our saints watch over us, turning observance into prayer on our behalf. Our family and friends weave in and out of our hours, noticing our demeanor, our habits, our moods. This attention can feel comforting and also smothering at times, especially when we've wandered off the path to Christ; when we'd prefer not to have other eyes upon us, their words sounding an alarm.

I was tromping across soggy ground in the wilds of Alaska, my friend Libby at my side. We were coming back to the hunting lodge from a long walk along the Cook Inlet, about a half mile to go. This landscape changed with the tides, trickling creeks swelling triple their size and back again throughout the day, and we were glad the water was low at that hour for easy crossings. Our lighthearted conversation halted as we heard the guide, there beside the lodge, screaming at us: "RUN! RUN!!!!"

Without looking behind us, or pausing to ask why we should do so, we broke into sprints, the grass slapping our shins as we tore through it. It is strange to run from an unknown danger, though in bear country it isn't difficult to deduce who our adversary was. We pounded up the steps, veritably flew through the open door, and he slammed the bear gate shut behind us.

Panting and wild-eyed, we turned to see two massive grizzly bears run into the yard, coming to a loping halt and sniffing the air, chuffing. We'd have died, it's as simple as that. We didn't know we were being tracked, but the guide had seen the bears following our scent across the tidal plain, and he'd seen us, completely oblivious to the danger we were in. He did everything he could to save our lives.

God has put, and will put, helpers on your journey, but you may not recognize them as such. Some will meekly suggest looking at something another way. Others may hurt you with a blunt rebuke. Some may very well scream at you to run from something or someone that threatens to destroy you. You must build up some toughness to let the pain of correction slide off of your heart while the truth is allowed to seep in and change you, rescue you. If the words are good but hurt, peek around on the other side of them to the love which pushed them forth. Give thanks for that love.

Not Consumed By Grizzlies,
Perseverance

WEEK THREE, DAY SIX

> "The heavens declare the glory of God;
> And the firmament shows His handiwork.
> Day unto day utters speech,
> And night unto night reveals knowledge.
> There is no speech nor language
> Where their voice is not heard.
> Their line has gone out through all the earth,
> And their words to the end of the world."
> Psalm 19:1-4

Dear Noticer,

It was near midnight on an island in Southern Chile, and we were camping out with our youth group when someone yelled out that the water of the bay was glowing. We ran down to the beach, and sure enough, wherever the water was stirred a bright green shone forth. It was bioluminescent plankton, which flash their lights brilliantly when disturbed. We ran for our bathing suits, jumped into the water, and swam through living light, gasping with wonder under the star-filled heavens.

Another time I was kneeling on the wet sand, digging for razor clams in Alaska, and had accidentally broken one with my shovel. I tossed it to the side of me and kept working. All of a sudden, I heard a whoosh of air and there, just feet from me, stood a bald eagle, eye-to-eye with me, leisurely enjoying the broken-open clam. I think I forgot how to breathe; the enormity and majesty of the bird was more than my mind could take in.

God placed Adam and Eve in a garden; they were surrounded by the beauty of plants and the companionship of the animals. Though they had to leave this verdant bower, our hearts have never stopped needing its gifts. Sunsets shot through with gold stop us in our tracks. The brilliant flashes of arcing lightning dazzle our eyes. Something within us responds to the woods cloaked in mist, the moss underfoot impossibly green, the deer pausing majestically before breaking into a run. As a cathedral is built to draw the parishioners' hearts upward in awe, so too this marvelous earth. Are we seeing?

God sends each of us the helpers unique to our lives and needs; for you it may not be an eagle in Alaska, but it may be the way your dog puts his head on your lap when you're sad. It may not be glowing plankton, but it could be a wildflower thriving defiantly in a sidewalk crack. Look about you while you journey, and let the beauty and wonder of His good creation draw you to the One who made it.

I leave you to ponder this quote from St. Basil the Great that always encourages me:

"When you look at the sky and the beauty of the stars, throw yourself at God's feet and adore Him who in His wisdom has arranged things in this way. Similarly, when the sun goes down and when it rises, when you are asleep or awake, give thanks to God, who created and arranged all things for your benefit, to have you know, love, and praise their Creator."

The Hugger of Trees,
Perseverance

WEEK THREE, DAY SEVEN
ADORATION OF THE CROSS

> *"Cast your burden on the Lord,*
> *And He shall sustain you;*
> *He shall never permit the righteous to be moved."*
> Psalm 55:22

Dear Burdened Heart,

Today's Divine Liturgy will take us back to last September when we celebrated the Exaltation of the Holy Cross, the day St. Helen found the very Cross of Christ and paraded it around the city, healing those its shadow fell upon. The prostrations and the songs will seem very familiar, as will the gilded cross standing before us for veneration. It is a reminder of our Lenten destination: Pascha is coming, though it is still many weeks away. But, before that glorious day arrives, we must face Holy Friday and Christ's crucifixion. Today we are called to ask ourselves if we will truly carry our own cross and follow Him through death.

This personal cross is also our companion on the journey. It is cumbersome and weighty, and we may often wonder how much easier our travels would be without it.

This cross can take many forms: a passion (misdirected strength) that is harder for us to tame than usual, a debilitating disorder or physical weakness, an illness of the mind, a frustrating relationship with a family member, a personality quirk, a lack of basic necessities, an oppressive culture, society, or government, or even martyrdom. This cross might be one we've picked up ourselves such an extra responsibility or volunteering to serve those we'd rather avoid. Many times, it's a cross placed upon us, one that we're born with or into, one that takes us by surprise and will not leave us no matter how hard we fight it.

This past week we've talked about the companions who help us on our path, and this companion is no different, though it is far less pleasant. Our goal of growing in Christ-likeness isn't an easy one. It requires a reshaping of our thoughts and feelings, and a scouring away of the disease of sin. Like weight-lifting strengthens our physical bodies, so also this cross strengthens our souls. It is often painful and tiring, but when we embrace it, we allow it to be used by God to help us grow more like Him, strengthening us in virtue.

All of the saints carried similar crosses that helped them to become the people of God that we know today. St. Paul writes in II Corinthians 12 about his "thorn in the flesh" which was meant to help him grow in humility. We don't know what exactly that thorn was, only that it bothered the Apostle so much that he begged God to take it from him. But God refused, saying instead, "My grace is sufficient for you, for My strength is made perfect in weakness." He says the same thing to us today about our own prickling companions. Is your cross feeling heavy today? Are you looking down the path of Lent wondering how you'll make it? As you bow toward Christ's own heavy cross today, recall those words to St. Paul and resolve to keep going, to see this through to the end, to walk through the valley of the shadow of death to the glorious resurrection that is to come. Believe it or not, your cross companion is helping you get there.

Carrying the Load With You,
Steadfast

WEEK FOUR: METHODS OF TRAVEL
SPIRITUAL DISCIPLINES TO STEADY OUR FEET

WEEK FOUR, DAY ONE

"Teach me Your way, O Lord;
I will walk in Your truth;
Unite my heart to fear Your name."
Psalm 86:11

Dear Empty Stomach,

"Who ate all the Pringles?!" My mom's voice yells across the house. "I just bought those!" My face goes pale. I thought I'd done a really good job of hiding the fact that I finished the entire can by myself, but apparently not. I was a young teen and no matter what time of day it was, I was hungry, especially in those hours between the end of school and dinner. The handful of chips Mom allowed me was never enough, so, I'd hid the can in my room and scarfed them all down, sneaking the empty can back into the trash can, hidden under piles of scrap paper in the hopes that no one would notice that I'd broken Mom's rules.

My sisters and I can still, to this day, recite the Food Creed: snack time is at 11am, 3pm, and 7pm. You are allowed only two cookies or a small handful of chips or a mouthful of crackers or a piece of Valentines/Halloween candy (when applicable). If dessert was to be had, it would be only after dinner and only if your plate was clean. Cake and ice cream were desserts, not snacks. No substitutions. No eating at odd times. You could skip a meal, but don't you dare add one. Why? Because it was WRONG. Snacks were BAD and UNHEALTHY. My transgression with the Pringles turned into an object lesson for my sisters who were instructed to never follow in my poor example. They would quickly rat me out if I did something as heinous as eat three Oreos instead of my allotted two (which, I confess, I also did often when I thought no one was looking). We were taught to push through the hunger in order to be perfect.

Perhaps your mother wasn't so strict, but I am under the impression that your perspective of food might be similar: it's a necessary evil. The line between too much and not enough is very narrow. One chip can tip the balance. One mouthful of ice cream can be unforgiveable. Skipping breakfast is commendable. How many calories can we intake without dying but still be considered beautiful, healthy, perfect? How close can we toe the line?

It should come as a shock to no one that my mother ended up in a hospital for anorexia. I can still remember clasping my arms around her in a hug and being able to grab my own elbows because of how thin she'd become. It was touch and go for a time, followed by weeks of inpatient therapy when we only got to see her maybe once or twice a month. My mother's food obsession nearly killed her.

So, fast forward many guilt ridden years of loving sweets and pizza, and I've been introduced to the concept of fasting. Yeah, ok, no biggie. Isn't that already my life? Watch what you eat and then you'll be perfect? I had all the wrong views of fasting: it'll make God love me, it'll make Him do what I want, or, worse yet, it'll help me stay skinny. This is not fasting. In fact, if you feel any of these things about fasting, don't do it. It took me many years to realize that fasting wasn't the answer to my perfection problem; it was the key to freedom from the fear of food.

What is food? At its core, all food comes from plants and animals that God created specifically for us. We thank God before we eat because all food is truly from Him. We depend on Him for our very substance. Our modern scene of fast food and instant noodles has hidden the miracle of food from our view, but just because we are blessed with it in abundance doesn't mean that food is less of a gracious gift. Food should point us to its source: God. It should remind us of His goodness and His care for us. Fasting is not a call to refrain from something bad. Food is good! God made it so! Fasting should remind us of that.

I look forward to fasting now because of how it heals my soul and helps me rediscover the blessing within God's gift of food. During Lent, I'm free of the food obsession my mother imparted to me. It's not about the rules. It's about God. We fast so that we can make room to pray. We fast to remind us of our dependence on God. We fast so that we can reorient ourselves and refocus our souls. After a few weeks into a fast, I'm no longer wistfully thinking about the foods I miss or complaining about the foods I'm eating. I'm just not thinking about food at all. But I am thinking about my body. I'm tuned in to its needs. I'm recognizing the signs that I'm lacking in protein or energy. Fasting means finding ways to meet those needs instead of just ignoring them like I tried to do (and failed at) as a kid. Lent is an endurance run, and to make it through I have to do the opposite of what most people think of when they hear the word "fasting": I need to care for my body, not ignore it like my mother did.

I was so skinny in high school that I wasn't allowed to donate blood. I went in and out of struggles with anemia. My heart felt like it was struggling just to pump. I thought ignoring my body's needs was good, but in God's eyes, I was doing damage to the body made in His image. Today, I'm a far cry from my high school weight, but according to my doctor, I'm as healthy as a horse. I didn't get that way by not eating, but by seeing food in a different light. Especially at the end of a fasting period, food becomes a celebration, a way to praise God for all His has done! Ice cream isn't evil, it's how I'm choosing to celebrate the Resurrection! I don't feel guilty about that! And during a fasting season, food becomes a way to reevaluate how I'm treating my body and how I'm viewing God and His gifts. Am I still obsessed with how much or little I eat? Is food still my focus? Or can I fast without doing damage to God's image (AKA, me)?

Maybe you can't fast like most other people do. Maybe it would be bad for your health or bad for your relationship with food (FYI: fasting actually won't make you skinny, trust me). But that's between you, your priest, your doctor, and God. Don't look at what other people are eating during this season. In fact, don't think too much about your own plate either. Fasting, at its core, is a weapon, strengthening you and training you to control your impulses. By temporarily (note that word please) saying no to what is good for us (AKA, certain foods), we are making it easier for ourselves to say no when we are tempted to lie, cheat, abuse another, gossip, steal, and use people for our gain, things that are actually evil. These are our true enemies during the fast: not food. So, whatever you do during Lent this year, do it for the glory of God, and do no harm to your body. Food is a tool not a tempter, and fasting is a discipline, not a diet plan.

Still Eating More Than Two Oreos,
Steadfast

WEEK FOUR, DAY TWO

> *"I will meditate on Your precepts,*
> *And contemplate Your ways.*
> *I will delight myself in Your statutes;*
> *I will not forget Your word."*
> Psalm 119:15-16

Dear Student of the Sacred,

Lent is traditionally the time when we re-devote ourselves to the practice of spiritual disciplines, namely the practices that those travelers way ahead of us on the road have already used and trust to get us safely to our destination. Fasting is one such discipline, and study of the Scriptures is another. If we are to continue on our way to God, the ancients make it clear that we must have a deep understanding of the Bible to guide us in His ways.

I know the Bible can seem intimidating, but, believe it or not, you are already learning the tools you need to accurately study it! Think of the English or Literature classes you have taken; these classes are teaching you how to study books by observing grammar, genre, setting, and symbolism. Some classes will have you focus on interpreting poetry. Your teachers are probably explaining the time period of the author and how that affects how you understand the story. Pay attention to what they tell you, because these are the very same tools you will use when studying the Bible.

The Bible is a book made up of many different books of all sorts of genres and from many different time periods. There are historical records, prophecies, books of poetry, letters, and narratives. It is full of symbolism, types and antitypes, cultural details, and apocalyptic imagery. Everything you learn in school about interpreting a classic applies also to Scripture. It is important to understand who wrote it, where, when, and why in order to understand its meaning. Because, unlike other books, this Book has a supernatural Source, the Holy Spirit. It is a Living Book, and proper study of it can yield an abundance of spiritual fruit in our lives.

But where to begin? As a teen, I realized that I had never before read the entire Bible, cover to cover, and I resolved to do just that. I wanted to become familiar with it in its entirety. Perhaps you'll want to attempt something similar, or perhaps you will want to start with the Gospels. Ask your priest for advice and, as you read, apply the methods you've used in school. If you run across something you don't understand, write it down. Check your church library for a commentary or ask your priest for help in finding the answers. You are not the first to dig for gold in God's Word; many have searched it out deeply and have left their wisdom behind for us to read in commentaries, study Bibles, or written homilies.

You can also get started with regular scripture readings without undertaking a large research and reading commitment. Look up an Orthodox daily readings app or website that tells you the scriptures, saint lives, and prayers for the day. Notice the patterns and objects that come up in the scripture readings at church, like water, trees, fruit, sweet ointments, deserts, Passover, redemption, and unexpected redirections and reversals. Do they come up in the hymns? Pay attention to those things that show up over and over again. Then look around you. Do you see them in your daily life? In the news? Stories you read for school? What about the lives of the saints? When you see a pattern or a symbol recurring, you know it's important. Make a note of it. You'll probably find that the meaning of that symbol or pattern is an important part of Holy Week and Pascha. If you train yourself now to notice the patterns, you'll be ready to see them when they appear in fullness.

Above all, do not lose heart. You are reading a book that was written thousands of years ago in languages you do not speak and in a culture you do not know. It's a daunting task, but God promises us an ally: His Spirit. Keep studying, asking questions, and seeking answers. The Holy Spirit will be forever guiding you to the truth.

Your Fellow Learner,
Steadfast

WEEK FOUR, DAY THREE

"Create in me a clean heart, O God,
And renew a steadfast spirit within me.
Do not cast me away from Your presence,
And do not take Your Holy Spirit from me."
Psalm 51:10-11

Dear Unashamed,

I was mortified. A high school classmate smiled and said, "That was so funny when you flashed everyone during the assembly." I stared at her thinking, unblinking, somehow choking out: "When I WHAT!?" Days had gone by, days since our cast had performed a small sampling from our upcoming show *Dancing at Lughnasa*, in full costume.

I wasn't aware that my dress flared out from my waist nearly parallel to the floor when I spun around during a scene. If I had known, I'd have worn shorts underneath, or at least not embarrassingly obvious polka dot underpants. My face burned with the fire of a thousand suns. I had basically de-pants-ed myself in front of the whole school. Suddenly a number of impudent smiles and comments of late made sense. Oh, God.

There have been so very many times in my life when I wanted to crawl under a table and hide from intense embarrassment, from shame. For a while it even kept me from seeking Christ; I felt that such a relationship was only for other, better people, not for the likes of me.

Remember the story of the woman who had the issue of blood for twelve years? She was living with intense shame because of her infirmity, as she was considered "unclean" and could not worship at the temple. We know her now as St. Veronica. So great was her faith that she was certain that even just touching the hem of Christ's garment would heal her. Christ felt the power go out from him, and asked who in the pressing crowd had touched him. She admitted her act, and He commended her saying, "Daughter, your faith has made you well. Go in peace, and be healed of your affliction."

Shame and embarrassment, whatever their sources, should never keep us from reaching out boldly for healing and forgiveness. The One who lovingly calls us "daughters" is able and willing to bring us to wholeness. Think of St. Veronica when you go to confess; go not with shame for how you're broken, but with faith for how He'll make you whole.

I want to leave you with a quotation from St. Silouan the Athonite that has comforted me since I read it. To me it tells more of the story of what happened to St. Veronica and what happens to us when we come to confession:

> "The Lord greatly loves the repenting sinner and mercifully presses him to His bosom: 'Where were you, My child? I was waiting a long time for you.'"

With Relief,
Perseverance

WEEK FOUR, DAY FOUR

*"Let my prayer be set before You as incense,
The lifting up of my hands as the evening sacrifice."*
Psalm 141:2

Dear Daughter of the Most High,

During my first few weeks at college, I found myself pouring out my heart to an upperclassman. I don't remember what was troubling me, but I felt overwhelmed and in need of help. He was very attentive and sympathetic, and, at the end of his reassurances, said, "I will absolutely be praying for you, and I mean it! I love to pray!" I was stunned. He loved to pray?! I could hardly believe it, except when I looked into his face, I could see his sincerity. He practically glowed when he spoke about prayer, as if he couldn't imagine anything he'd rather be doing. Decades later, I still wish I had that same love and zeal.

I struggled constantly with prayer. Unlike my friend the upperclassman, I found it boring. I'm a person of action. Stopping to pray just never occurred to me and even then, what should I say? Yet I knew that monks, nuns, and even your average church-goer dedicate hours to prayer, convinced of its vital power to help in every circumstance. I resolved after that conversation to get more serious about praying, to form a sort of "prayer rule." A rule in this sense means a set of daily goals and habits, patterns that fit into your regular life and help you notice God's presence with you. After my talk with the boy who loved to pray, I decided to pray every morning and every night.

It took a lot of practice and patience and working through days and nights when I just did not want to pray before I noticed a change in myself. I started to reach for prayer as a needed part of my day. Though I struggle with meaningful, focused prayer, and though I lack the exuberance of my friend, something in my soul groans when I do not pray. It is a tangible, empty feeling.

But why set aside time to talk with God when God is always around me, already knows what I need or what I might say? Because I need prayer to thrive. To pray is to accept God's loving invitation to speak to Him face to face. We read in Exodus that speaking to God made Moses' face shine so much that he needed a veil! We cannot speak to God and come away unchanged, even if we don't notice the change at first. After finding the prayers of the Church and praying them regularly for years, I have come to rely on them as starting points for helping me find the right words to express my thoughts and feelings to God.

Do you have a prayer rule (a pattern of prayer set into your daily life)? Lent is a great time to start if you do not. If you aren't currently following a prayer rule, talk with your priest and come up with one that best suits you. You'll be surprised how much difference it can make to shape your day around a few simple prayers such as The Our Father, the Trisagion, "Lord, have mercy," and the Jesus Prayer.

I wonder what it would be like to invite God in as you brush your teeth, sit in class, watch a movie, or talk with a friend? He is always there, of course, but we often ignore Him. How would my life change if I were constantly praying, constantly focused on God, constantly looking for Him to act? The possibilities are endless. Perhaps, Lord willing, we will discover them!

Praying With You,
Steadfast

WEEK FOUR, DAY FIVE

Lord, who may abide in Your tabernacle?
Who may dwell in Your holy hill?
He who walks uprightly,
And works righteousness,
And speaks the truth in his heart,
He who does not backbite with his tongue,
Nor does evil to his neighbor,
Nor does he take up a reproach against his friend."
Psalm 15:1-3

Dear Caretaker of Words,

It's an easy and terrible habit. Gossiping about others and criticizing them seems as natural as breathing. We've all been hurt when careless and cutting words have made their way to our ears, especially if they were spoken behind our backs by people we like. We've winced when someone we love is spoken about in a harsh or condemning way.

    A few decades ago, I had a friend who was often disparaged in conversation in our circle. The person had a difficult temperament to be sure, but I felt guilty of betrayal when I participated in gossiping, and I wanted no more part in the dismissive shakes of the heads and sighs of superiority. I imagined myself in that person's shoes with all that derision directed at me. How horrid! I decided to try an experiment.

My experiment was to see if I could make a difference by not only never uttering an unkind thing about this person, but further, to say something that was worthy about them instead. This went on for only a few weeks before I began to see the softening towards this person among our group. Soon the negative words stopped. I realized that we rarely repeat actions that are not affirmed by those closest to us; for instance, if no one laughs at a racist joke or a fat joke, it's unlikely another will be tried out. That is the power of not smiling and nodding. That is the power of silence, and further, of redirection.

It matters how we talk about our fellow pilgrims. Our words shape not only the opinions and actions of others, but also our own hearts. Can we with one tongue cut apart our brother, and then ask for our Lord's mercy for ourselves? The Bible often refers to the tongue as being a small thing of great import (the rudder of a ship, a spark that can ignite a fire). Controlling our tongues, our words, is a spiritual discipline that will aid us greatly, all out of proportion to its size.

My experiment continues on to the present. I have found that one of the gifts of trying not to speak ill of others is that you become a safe person to confide in. People can share what they're going through, because they know their words won't be carried to unintended ears, won't be dissected by the opinions of others. Let us journey well together, binding up one another's wounds, rather than picking them open.

Still Learning,
Perseverance

WEEK FOUR, DAY SIX

"Blessed is he who considers the poor;
The Lord will deliver him in time of trouble.
The Lord will preserve him and keep him alive,
And he will be blessed on the earth"
Psalm 41:1-2

Dear Compassionate Friend,

The layout of my high school was unusual. Because we lived in sunny Florida, the hallways were mostly outdoors. Instead of one large, multi-story building, we had many one-story buildings spread across the campus with grass fields and open pathways between them. It was refreshing to be able to go outdoors as you walked between classes...except for when it rained. Though rare, the typical Florida rainstorm was a monsoon. Walls of water would suddenly fall from the sky, instantly drenching anyone unlucky enough to not have sufficient cover.

It was one such rainy morning that I found myself in a predicament: I needed to cross an open space to get to my next class. I didn't have a raincoat or hood, and I was sure to be soaked. I stood there at the edge of the awning calculating my next move. Should I wait for the rain to slow? Did I have time? Should I run for it? At that moment, a fellow student, whom I'd never seen before, came up to me holding an umbrella. "Do you need to get across?" he asked me. I nodded emphatically. "Here. I'll walk you over." And just like that, he held his umbrella over my head and kept me dry as we went across. "Thank you!" I said as we made it to the next overhang. He smiled, and I watched him walk back across the field and approach another student waiting where I had been.

It suddenly occurred to me that this total stranger was willingly giving up his time to help walk people across the field with his umbrella. He didn't need to. He could have kept his umbrella to himself and gotten to his next class dry and on time. But he chose to wait and help those like myself who were not prepared for the sudden storm. It was a small act of kindness that made a huge impression on me.

Almsgiving is considered a major spiritual discipline (practice that teaches you to recognize and imitate God) in the Church. Both the Scriptures and the Church Fathers repeatedly urge us to consider the poor and needy, giving freely and often. Today, when we hear the word "almsgiving", we almost always think of money, but what that student gave to me that rainy morning was just as valuable. Out of his abundance (in this case, his umbrella) he gave to those of us who had nothing. Almsgiving doesn't always have to be about money. It could be giving of your time, your things, your abilities, a listening ear, an extra pencil during a test, a kind word, a helping hand.

Take stock of what God has given you. What do you have that you could share with those in need? As you walk about your day, look around and notice what's going on. Is there someone in need? Is God nudging you to give of yourself to help a friend, teacher, sibling, parent, or passerby? Don't be afraid to think creatively, and don't fall into the trap of thinking that your offering is too small. All that student had was an umbrella, but his kindness changed my life.

Blessed and Dry,
Steadfast

WEEK FOUR, DAY SEVEN
SUNDAY OF ST. JOHN CLIMACUS

But You, O Lord, are a shield for me,
My glory and the One who lifts up my head.
I cried to the Lord with my voice,
And He heard me from His holy hill.
Psalm 3:3-4

Dear White-Knuckled Climber,

As you walked into church today, perhaps you noticed the unusual icon depicting a long ladder stretching from earth to Heaven, people ascending, demons attacking the climbers with arrows, hooks, and all manner of weaponry, sometimes even succeeding in making them fall, and at the top, Christ, His arms extending in welcome.

St. John Climacus, or St. John of the Ladder, was a monk in the 6th century who wrote The Ladder of Divine Ascent for his brother monks; it's a treatise about detaching from sinful passions (misdirected strengths) and progressing from virtue to virtue, arriving at salvation. Though his book was written for monastics, the truths he expressed are helpful to each layperson as well.

St. John Climacus gave this advice that has stuck with me whenever I am tempted to be discouraged by my own weakness: "Do not be surprised that you fall every day; do not give up, but stand your ground courageously. And assuredly, the angel who guards you will honor your patience."

This past week we've looked at the disciplines that help keep our feet on the path, on the rungs of the ladder. Think of the icon; it is certainly true. Christ does await us in glory, and demons do indeed assault us as we work out our salvation. Some of us fall, some persist. We have the work of moving our grip from rung to rung, virtue to virtue.

But Christ isn't just at the top of the ladder. We have help all along the way.

I was nervous the night before we were received into the Orthodox Church. Would I goof up? Say or do something wrong? Our calm Khouria (priest's wife) allayed my fears, reminding me that I wasn't coming to "do something", but to "receive something." I needed to be ready to receive; that was all. Christ was coming down the ladder to me, to us. In the sacraments, He draws near, filling the natural with the supernatural, the created with the uncreated, and we receive Him in a mystery.

Baptism, chrismation, communion, holy orders, confession, anointing of the sick, and marriage are sacraments; they are all guaranteed places to meet God in holy encounters (though of course He does not limit Himself to these). He does not passively wait for us at the top of the ladder. He actively comes down to meet us where we are, to strengthen us for the climb, to heal our infirmities both spiritual and physical, and to bind the earthly with the Heavenly.

By His Strength, Climbing,
Perseverance

WEEK FIVE: REST FOR THE WEARY
COMFORT IN THE MIDST OF HARD TRAVEL

WEEK FIVE, DAY ONE

> *"I will lift up my eyes to the hills—*
> *From whence comes my help?*
> *My help comes from the Lord,*
> *Who made heaven and earth."*
> Psalm 121:1-2

Dear Scaler of Heights,

One of my favorite childhood vacation spots was a tiny cabin in the middle of the Pennsylvania Appalachians. My grandparents would often take us there where we'd catch crawfish in the creek and keep our eyes open for black bear. At some point in the week, Grandpa would lead us hiking up one of the mountains. It was a long, sometimes difficult trek through uncharted woods, clinging to walking sticks for balance as we trod uphill. When he'd announce that we were at the top, I'd always be surprised!

The top of a mountain never looks how you'd imagine as a kid. It's almost indistinguishable from the rest of the mountain except the slope isn't as pronounced. I'd fall on top of a log, gasping for breath after the hike, looking around and just reveling in the fact that I was at the top, even if it didn't seem that special. I often had no idea where we were headed, but Grandpa always knew the way. As long as I was following him, we'd get there and back again.

We are now over halfway through Lent. One could say that we've reached the summit of the fast. It probably doesn't feel that special or different. In fact, you might be feeling tired, worn out from the strictness of the spiritual climb. That's okay. Lent is not meant to be easy. We are readying ourselves for the celebration of all celebrations, recognizing the ultimate victory and sacrifice of our faith. The preparations for our soul take time and grit. We know that joy is coming, that we've made it this far, but right now the top of the mountain doesn't feel much different from the bottom.

Looking back, we've come a long way from that first exciting week when our journey was still new. We've gone through pitfalls and temptations, found companions for the road, and sought out various methods and disciplines to help us on our way. Looking ahead, there are dragons lurking before we get to the deep darkness of the Holy Week vigil, culminating in that long Saturday of silence and waiting before the burst of light that is Pascha. But all of that is to come. For now, we want to take a breath, sit on our logs, and regain our strength. As I learned hiking with Grandpa, it's the descent that is the hardest, not the initial climb. Lent will get harder before it gets easier. It's ok to take things slower right now and pace yourself.

This week we'll focus on the things that give us comfort, the ways that God encourages us when the journey is long and we still have far to go. If you're in need of solace, you're not alone. We are walking this difficult journey with you, and we know it can be rough. But we also know that, just like during my hikes with Grandpa, we have a Guide Who knows where He's taking us, even if right now we're questioning whether the struggle is worth it.

Just a little farther now. Sit down. Rest. Have a cool drink of water for your soul, and take in the view.

Sitting By Your Side,
Steadfast

WEEK FIVE, DAY TWO

> *"Blessed is he whose transgression is forgiven,*
> *Whose sin is covered."*
> Psalm 32:1-2

Dear Irreplaceable,

Lifting the nesting box lid, I spoke with my hen Sam, who poofed her feathers protectively. She'd been broody for months, trying to mother infertile eggs, so I'd given her some fertile ones from a friend who had a rooster in her flock. I wrote the due date on the calendar and checked on her regularly to make sure she was still devoted to the job. Two days from the due date I decided to candle an egg to see if she had been able to keep them alive. What a wonder to hear, right through the shell, little peeping sounds! Hens and chicks form a bond even before hatching, mama reassuringly clucking so the little ones know her voice.

This verse (Matthew 23:37) comes at the end of a long upbraiding of the priests, scribes, and Pharisees:

> "O Jerusalem, Jerusalem, the one who kills the
> prophets and stones those who are sent to her! How
> often I wanted to gather your children together, as a

hen gathers her chicks under her wings, but you were not willing!"

Jesus pulled no punches. He called them hypocrites, white washed tombs, and a brood of vipers. Our Lord knew all of the worst about His children, and yet what he ends with is the most tender of images: a hen protectively gathering her chicks beneath her wings. I thought of Sam, forgoing food, water, and bathroom breaks for hours on end, fiercely protecting her little clutch with aggressive clucks and poofed feathers.

Peeps (baby chicks) are disasters without caregivers. They wander out, vulnerable to hawks. They foul their drinking water and food. They fall into water and get dangerously chilled. They even need their feces washed off of their bums at times to prevent a life-threatening blockage. Taking care of them is no small job, and by extension, taking care of us isn't either!

I held the chirping egg in my hand, the warmth of it radiating through my skin. I returned it with wonder to Sam, tucking it below her. The Lord, the Creator of the heavens and the earth compared Himself to a hen. He mourned His children's estrangement from Him with humble love. He openly grieved that they would not be gathered, would not be protected, would not entrust themselves to Him.

Bad and unmanageable as they were, they were His, and He wanted them. He wants us too. Our stupidities, our selfishness, our mistakes, our wounds, none of these are impediments to His ever-wild, untamable love. This is the very best of news.

God's Mess and Delight,
Perseverance

WEEK FIVE, DAY THREE

"Whenever I am afraid,
I will trust in You.
In God (I will praise His word),
In God I have put my trust;
I will not fear.
What can flesh do to me?"
Psalm 56:3-4

Dear Child of God,

There was a time in my life when I was a competitive rower in Chile. The boats we raced were long and skinny, with gigantic oars stretched out like agile wings. Normally I competed in a double, my partner and I moving as one unit as we rolled our seats forward, dug in our oars, and used every major muscle group to propel backward across the water.

My trainer announced to me that he intended to teach me sweeping, where each rower uses one big oar each rather than two. I was pretty shaky as we pulled away from the floating dock; it's not unlike switching from skiing to snowboarding, and none of my skills were transferring easily. We rowed toward the middle of the canal, barely managing to synchronize our strokes, when he suddenly yelled, "NOW! ROW! FASTER! NOW!"

"I am not ready for sprints; what is he thinking?" I thought as I looked over my shoulder to check our direction. All I could see was blue, the sheer, steep, ascending prow of a ferry. My mind registered that it was about to cut our boat in half, the V-shape slicing through the water with hungry immediacy. I threw myself body and soul into my strokes, leaning every muscle and tendon into a frantic bid for survival. We barely pulled the last few inches away from the prow before it charged past, the wall of the ship skimming the tips of our oars as we tried to stay upright on the peaks of the waves.

A deckhand on the back of the ship saw us and blanched white. They'd had no idea we were there; they had abruptly course corrected to avoid a small water taxi, leaving us in their blind spot. We were nearly propeller fodder, our strapped-in feet and delicate boat were a recipe for death in such a collision.

As much as we prepare and plan, there will come times in your pilgrimage when you have to do things that you don't feel at all prepared to do. It would be nice if we always felt equipped and competent beforehand, but we do serve a God who seems to delight in seeing us rise to the challenges we were convinced were out of our reach, impossible. As my coach did, He gives us the directions we need in the moment we need them.

Are you holding back from something that you know God is inviting you to do? It can be as simple as reaching out to a shy, awkward kid at youth group and including them. Maybe saying yes to a camp counselor position, or applying to that esteemed university that rejects most applicants? Hard, seemingly impossible things are catalysts for growth.

Somehow Still Alive,
Perseverance

WEEK FIVE, DAY FOUR

> "He makes me to lie down in green pastures;
> He leads me beside the still waters.
> He restores my soul"
> Psalm 23:2-3

My Dear Tired Soul,

When I was in my first trimester, nauseated and tired as I grew a child within me, my father was in a terrible car accident and suddenly needed someone to care for him. My younger sisters and I spent day after day in a hospital for the better part of a month. Between that, working remotely, and morning sickness, I was constantly exhausted and depressed. My husband was across the country, and my sisters and I were too frazzled to be much emotional support to each other. Fortunately, a dear friend read between the lines of my social media updates and knew I was taxed. She dropped everything and rushed to my aid.

My sisters were gracious enough to give me the day off. I jumped into this friend's car, and she sped me away. We had lunch, saw a movie, ate ice cream, and just talked.

I didn't need to rush to a hospital or type any e-mails or drag my weary body anywhere. She cared for me and gave me the break I needed. I returned home feeling well-loved and refreshed. Nothing had changed; I was still pregnant and weak, my dad was still recovering, and my job still needed me. But I had renewed strength to face those challenges.

A journey is a tiring experience, especially when it is long. If you've ever hiked a long trail or gone on a cross-country road trip, you know that you can't just start out and go full-speed until your journey is done. You need breaks. You need pit stops. Life is much the same way. It is a long, tiring journey, and there will be times you will need to stop and rest in order to have the strength to go on. Please know, that's entirely ok. God made the world with Sabbath rest built in. He knows we need rest.

Many times in the Gospels, we see Jesus taking a break, going away to pray, or even sleeping. The Son of God needed rest. Do we think we're any better than He? The Sabbath or Day of Rest is holy to God, and rest should be holy to us, too. Not getting enough rest leads to burnout, making you ineffective for the road, unable to finish the trail.

Whatever you're facing today, give yourself permission to rest. In this frantic, busy culture, know that it is ok to stop and catch your breath. Maybe that looks like a nap, a movie, a walk in nature, a vacation, a game, reading, playing music–whatever helps you to refresh and refocus. This journey, especially during Lent, is hard on body and soul. Go easy. Check your pace. The road will still be here when you're ready.

Your Kindred Spirit,
Steadfast

WEEK FIVE, DAY FIVE

> "Hear my cry, O God;
> Attend to my prayer.
> From the end of the earth I will cry to You,
> When my heart is overwhelmed;
> Lead me to the rock that is higher than I.
> For You have been a shelter for me,
> A strong tower from the enemy.
> I will abide in Your tabernacle forever;
> I will trust in the shelter of Your wings."
> Psalm 61:1-4

Dear Learner,

I remember crying over algebra homework. The combined pressure of school, work, sports, youth group, and theatre was intense to begin with, but when something went wrong, there wasn't enough time, energy, or emotional reserves left to spare. The years have not made me forget that helpless and overwhelmed feeling, the dread that this, right now, is the very moment when I shall ruin my life, miss my chance, and end up a failure. I am old enough now to watch my own teens go through it.

I might not have known that God cares for all of our worries—even my homework anxieties—if it hadn't been for a pair of boots. We'd been invited to an outdoor winter wedding ceremony, which put me into a conundrum. I should wear a dress, but I had no dressy boots to go with it. Money was very tight, so there'd be no shopping for some, but I couldn't wrap my mind around wearing my sturdy snow boots with a dress. The day before the wedding I prayed for boots as I showered. After getting dressed I checked my messages and saw that a family member wanted to know if I'd like a pair of dress boots that they'd found in a storage unit. They were beautiful, and they were my size.

But I might not have fully gotten the message that God takes care of us if it hadn't been for the mascara, yes, Providential Mascara. I don't wear much makeup, but I do apply mascara to my very light lashes so that my eyes can function with less glare and show up in photos. It was another season when money was tight, and my mascara was hopelessly dried out. I took a walk with my daughter, and as we crossed a bridge, I spied something in the gutter. I bent to pick it up: it was a brand-new mascara, still in the sealed, though scuffed-up, packaging! God had provided even mascara!

God is very near us, always. He cares about our anxieties, our stress, our depression, and our material needs and wants. He delights in being invited into all of it; He knows what to do with our mess, our tears, and our ills. He knows what we need, when we need it, and why. He does not give us everything we want, but what He knows sets us up best to know Him. Sometimes, that's a gift as small as a mascara.

Under His Mercy,
Perseverance

WEEK FIVE, DAY SIX

> "I will meditate on the glorious splendor of Your majesty,
> And on Your wondrous works."
>
> Psalm 145:5

Dear Frantic Mind,

I struggle with racing thoughts and an anxious brain. There is so much to do, so much pressure to perform, so many voices in my head crying and screaming in need or judgment. Many times, I've wished to shut them up, to be able to focus and rest in the moment without the fear that I'm wasting time or skimping on my to-do list. I yearn for peace in the deepest parts of my being, but in this racing age of instant communication, cross-ocean travel, and deadlines, it almost feels impossible.

    At one point, I wasn't able to sleep well at night. My thoughts would race and churn, jumping between moments in the past to tasks for the future, to the creeping worries and fears I tried to lock away under my bed. I complained to my therapist, and she recommended I try doing "mindfulness exercises" before I go to bed each night. I did, and they helped tremendously!

"Mindfulness," when you truly boil it down, is simply a modern psychology term for "meditation," the ancient practice of focusing on your breath and perhaps one or two phrases over and over again as a way to still your mind. To many people, this sounds like a foreign concept perhaps adopted from some ancient pagan religion, but actually this idea of meditation was endorsed by the early Christian Church as a prayerful means of quieting ourselves and listening for God's still, small voice.

The prayer ropes many Orthodox Christians wear function as aids in this important practice. Meditative prayer is easy to do, but hard to maintain. Often our minds are not used to rest and inactivity. But this stillness is necessary if we are to obtain equilibrium in a world of screaming madness.

Find a comfortable place to sit or a quiet path to walk, turn off your phone, hold a prayer rope in your hand if you have one, and take a very deep breath in and then slowly let it out. For each breath, touch a bead or knot on your rope and say the name, Jesus. You can also speak the full Jesus prayer softly as you breathe ("Lord Jesus Christ, have mercy on me."), or recite a short Bible verse (such as one of the Psalms in this book) over and over as you move your fingers along the knots. When thoughts come, as they will, acknowledge them, and gently let them go. Don't worry about performance or "doing it right." Just breathe. Offer the moment to Jesus. Be still, or walk slowly. Don't focus on any anxious voices in your head, but offer them to God as you say Jesus' name and ask His mercy. Wait on God and His soothing presence.

I am making this letter brief in the hopes that you will use the time set aside to read to try a little meditative prayer for at least five minutes. If you can make time to do it every day, even for just a little bit, both the psychologists and the saints can attest that it will greatly aid you as you listen for God and seek to embrace peace in a community of chaos. May your meditation be blessed.

Breathing Deeply,
Steadfast

WEEK FIVE, DAY SEVEN
SUNDAY OF ST. MARY OF EGYPT

"The sacrifices of God are a broken spirit,
A broken and a contrite heart—
These, O God, You will not despise"
Psalm 51:17

Dear Repentant One,

She was different from all the other women saints. Where they were covered in flowing robes, she was nearly naked. Where their hair was tidy and tucked under mantles, hers was wild, choppy, and bleached by the sun. "Who is she?" my heart asked, my eyes returning to her after surveying the iconography in the nave. "Who is this wild woman?"

In the fourth century, after leaving home for Alexandria at the tender age of twelve, Mary entered into a life of sensuality, using sex as entertainment and a way to have power over men. She lived as a slave to her shameful habits, which she described as an out of control need to use her strength to lie in filth, for seventeen years. She begged and spun flax for her income, and constantly sought to satisfy her relentless desires: Sex, wine, music, and excitement were her drugs of choice. One day she saw a group of men who were making a pilgrimage to Jerusalem to venerate the True Cross. She offered her body as payment for her passage, determined to accompany them. We don't know why she wished to make the journey–a pilgrimage no less–but God did, and He was drawing our wild mother to Himself.

At the door of the church, she tried to enter, but a force held her back. She realized that her sins were preventing her from approaching the Life-Giving Cross. She withdrew to a portico and saw an icon of the Holy Theotokos (Mother of God). It was there, friend, that she broke. She repented of her wanton life, and asked the help of the Mother of God to be able to enter the church and see the cross of her Son. She vowed that she would never again defile herself with fornication, and feeling the compassion of the Holy Theotokos, she was able to enter. There she heard, "If you cross the Jordan, you will find glorious rest."

After receiving the lifegiving mysteries, our wild mother left all that she knew. Guided by the Holy Theotokos, Mary entered a life of repentance in the desert for forty-eight years, her clothing disintegrating off of her body, subsisting on herbs and whatever she could forage. St. Zosimas found her, and we know her story of deep repentance through him. She addressed him by name before they had spoken. She lifted up off the ground when she prayed. When she needed to cross a river, she crossed herself and walked atop the water. She quoted scripture, though she had never read or heard it read. She was a far different Mary than the one who'd joined the band of pilgrims, looking for some fun.

Mary followed the promise and found "glorious rest" in the extremes of the desert: blaring sun and heat by day, wild beasts, cold by night, no clothing to mitigate those extremes. In all of her miseries, God never abandoned her; by them in fact was He redirecting her wayward desires, healing her wounds, and saving her. What looked like a place of deprivation, became for her a place of solace. Rest will not always look comfortable, and the good way will not always look inviting, but let us follow St. Mary, further up, further in.

By Her Prayers,
Perseverance

WEEK SIX: HERE THERE BE DRAGONS
WHEN OUR JOURNEY IS TREACHEROUS

WEEK SIX, DAY ONE

> *"Blessed be the Lord,*
> *Who has not given us as prey to their teeth.*
> *Our soul has escaped as a bird from the snare of the fowlers;*
> *The snare is broken, and we have escaped."*
> Psalm 124:6-7

Dear Valiant Heroine,

We have come to the sixth week of Lent. I have always found this week to be the most difficult. Pascha is almost here, but not yet. You can dream of the foods to come, but cannot taste them. The fatigue and frustration with being so close and yet so far starts to make this last leg of the journey almost unbearable. You can see the destination, can almost touch it! But you still have so far to go. During this tough week, we want to also focus on some of the hardest challenges of our pilgrimage to Christ: the dragons that bar our path and threaten our very life and soul.

    One such dragon that is far too common is abuse. Emotional, physical, spiritual, sexual, whatever sinister form it takes, abuse of all kinds is a terrifying dragon that stands in our path, setting us aflame with its terrible breath, leaving us worn, withered, and wounded beyond measure. If you have not encountered this dragon, chances are that you know someone who has, though perhaps they haven't openly shared about it yet. Shame and abuse often walk hand in hand.

I have stared down the dragon of abuse many, many times. My childhood was full of it, coming from a mother who was deeply disturbed and took every opportunity to tear down her children. It was a battle that would wage for years, and I emerged from that atmosphere in bad shape. My sense of self was shattered, my emotions were in turmoil, and I was easy prey for others to maim and manipulate. I didn't know what was happening to me, and I blamed myself for not being strong enough, good enough, smart enough, etc. I thought my pain was my fault.

If you are an abuse victim, I want you to hear this from someone who knows what you're feeling: this is not your fault. You were made in the very image of God, and nothing gives anyone the right to do violence to that sacred image. I don't care what you said, where you were, what you wore, what you did or didn't do. Abuse is never deserved, and the devil compounds your pain by making you think that it is, keeping you in a state of defeat. This monster in our path is enormous and well armored. We cannot fight it alone, and we shouldn't try. Chances are, you have come away from that battle with wounds so deep, you cannot possibly go on without being healed.

Thankfully, God provides healing, including in the work of good therapists who can help you put your pieces back together and find the strength to keep going. Don't be afraid to reach out for help. Find someone that makes you feel safe such as a teacher, priest, parent, or friend, preferably an adult who can help protect you if necessary. Find healing, and call in reinforcements.

If you are not an abuse victim, resolve to become a safe person. Ask the safe people in your life, such as your priest and parents and godparents, for advice. Ask them how you might listen and be hospitable to a friend who has survived abuse. Most of all, pray for survivors. You don't have to have all the answers. Sometimes the best thing you can do is encourage someone to get help and stay by their side as they do so. This dragon may be fearsome, but by working together, with God's help, it can be overcome.

Fighting with You,
Steadfast

WEEK SIX, DAY TWO

> *"Because he has set his love upon Me,*
> *therefore I will deliver him;*
> *I will set him on high, because he has known My name.*
> *He shall call upon Me, and I will answer him;*
> *I will be with him in trouble;*
> *I will deliver him and honor him."*
> Psalm 91:14-15

Dear Pestered One,

We are currently experiencing a moth infestation, which is as horrible as it sounds. I am a beekeeper, and I keep some of my empty hive equipment in our unfinished basement. Wax moths love such conditions when they can happen upon them, and happily took over the bee boxes. We came home one evening to moths in all the places. Reading a book by a lamp is hazardous; one will be dive-bombed by multiple moths, which for me results in undignified screaming and flailing.

Like these maddening moths, so too our hearts can be plagued and pestered by intrusive and unrelenting thoughts. When I was a young teen experiencing social volatility in my group of friends and stress from school work, I was often visited by a thought that it would be so much better to die rather than to live. Whenever life seemed impossibly hard, the thought would come creeping into the room of my heart, draw close behind me, and whisper convincingly. The Enemy attempts to make his confusing and misleading words indistinguishable from our own thoughts by hiding among them.

The enemy is very fond of shooting at us through thoughts; he pays attention to which ones we bring into the room of our hearts, cradling them in our arms, and leaning into them. He also notes which ones we brush off, which ones don't even have the enticement to merit a response. He is a skilled archer and a relentless one. Like the endless moths fluttering past my face, so do thoughts full of envy, hate, anger, bitterness, and greed assault me. St. Porphyrios once said, "When a bad or gloomy thought, fear, or temptation threatens to afflict you, don't fight it to try and get rid of it. Open your arms to Christ's love and He will embrace you, then it will vanish by itself."

I didn't know back then that the suicidal thoughts were coming at me from the outside, that they were intruders, arrows meant to strike me down. But I know now that there is a great deal I can do to guard my thoughts. I can memorize prayers and scriptures that tell me the truth so that I can recognize the lies and fight them when they fly at me. If a suicidal thought attacks, like a moth it will burn up in the flame of the promise of God, "I shall not die, but live, And declare the works of the Lord" (Psalm 118:17). I can remember that I am the doorkeeper of my thoughts, standing like a wizard to challenge anything that might enter, and telling the bad thoughts, "You shall not pass." The challenge questions are simple: Is it good? Is it admirable? Is it true? Is it of Christ?

When we lived in Chile, we could hear earthquakes coming across the landscape, shaking the trees, before we ever felt the earth move under our feet. So too with being watchful over our thoughts; with practice you can hear the arrow splitting the air, and you can brace yourself, raising the shield of prayer.

Swatting Moths and Intrusive Thoughts,
Perseverance

WEEK SIX, DAY THREE

"Answer me speedily, O Lord;
My spirit fails!
Do not hide Your face from me,
Lest I be like those who go down into the pit."
Psalm 143:7

Dear Sorrowful Eyes,

Tenth grade was probably one of the darkest years of my life. I was at the bottom, depressed, despairing of all life. I felt degraded in my home, torn apart by people who were supposed to be my friends, and utterly devoid of hope. It was why I suddenly found myself at this birthday party, where I hardly knew anyone. It was a raucous occasion, full of sensuality. I found myself whirling in the middle of it all, being pawed over and kissed and drowning in all the sensations. There was a warning light in my head. I knew where this could end. I had always devoted myself to God, had resolved to save myself for marriage, but when the suggestion was made to turn this birthday party into a sleepover, I agreed to it, knowing full well that my virginity was in danger. But I was dying in the pit of anguish, and nothing mattered to me anymore.

Despair is such a wretched beast. It tears away at every foundation, causing you to lose the strength to fight off the devils that you had so easily trampled underfoot once before. It hides your view of the Destination; it binds your will and breaks your spirit. Within me was no vagrant sexual desire. I didn't even care about these people. But they wanted me, though only my body, and it was more than anyone else seemed to care about at that time, so I passively let myself go. I gave myself up to the monster, no longer able to fight it.

God, however, did not stop fighting for me. That evening, while others engaged in their sexual activities, I found myself weeping in the arms of a girl I'd only just met. She stroked my hair and comforted me the entire night, and I left the party unscathed and miraculously renewed with just the tiniest sliver of hope to sustain me another day. God intervened and sent this girl to me, because He knew that the sensual activities were ultimately not what I wanted. In fact, now that I'm married, I realize what I was rescued from.

Sex is binding. While our culture tries to downplay its spiritual and emotional significance, in reality giving your body to another creates a deep spiritual bond that you can tangibly feel. It's exhilarating when it's with someone you want to love and cherish forever, but when it happens casually, with a stranger, the results are devastating. If I had let myself be taken advantage of at that party, my despair would only have grown. I would've found myself bound to someone I didn't know and barely liked. My spirit would have been in more anguish than it currently was. I might've broken beyond the point of no return.

The demon of despair lurks and preys upon many, especially the young. If it can grab you now, it can easily continue to hound you, wrecking your life and leading you to where you do not wish to be. But God is your Hero and Protector. Cry out, scream for Him to help you. Or, if you lack even the ability to do that, ask others to call out for you. The girl I met at that party was a Christian. I've no doubt she was praying for me that night even while I lacked the strength to do so myself. Hold on. Help is coming.

Rescued and Redeemed,
Steadfast

WEEK SIX, DAY FOUR

"He shall cover you with His feathers,
And under His wings you shall take refuge;
His truth shall be your shield and buckler.
You shall not be afraid of the terror by night,
Nor of the arrow that flies by day,
Nor of the pestilence that walks in darkness,
Nor of the destruction that lays waste at noonday."
Psalm 91:4-6

Dear On Guard,

My husband and I were overseas missionaries for many years in Chile. We regularly met for Bible study with teens from my rowing club. At one point, demons came up in our conversation, and I asked if anyone in the group had experienced an encounter with such a being. Every hand raised, and I realized that the enemy works in whatever way is most effective in each particular culture. In first world countries he tends to hide. There where we were, he frightens out in the open. Some shared how they'd watched dark beings crawl up their walls and across their ceilings. Others had been sat on and felt crushed and unable to breathe.

We, too, experienced this. One night I awoke to a dark presence in our bedroom, right on the ceiling over our bed. I cannot quite articulate the horror and ugliness hovering there, sucking the light and life from the room, but I curled up and prayed, and quickly it fled away. Within a minute all three of my children awoke from their sleep crying, one mumbling fearfully, "I don't know what it is!!" As frightening as it was, we could see so clearly that Christ was far more powerful than the demon.

Another time my neighbor asked me to come over to pray with her as her son had been seeing an evil presence walking in their upstairs rooms. We left our kids to play together as we went up and closed the door to pray without their noise. As soon as I began to pray something banged into the closed door from the other side with tremendous force, causing us both to jump and scream. Thinking that of course one of the children had fallen into the door we immediately swung it open to help them, but there was nobody there. The children were still playing downstairs. The demonic presence in the home did not want us praying!

As Orthodox Christians, we received the Holy Spirit in baptism, and we touch the very Body and Blood of Christ when we go to Communion. St. John Chrysostom tells us that we participate in Baptism and Communion, lightning shoots out from our faces to repel demons. But even so, we have to fight the spiritual fight until our last breath. Thankfully, we can make the sign of the Cross, look towards and kiss our holy icons, and ask our patron saints for help each day, whether we feel and see the encroaching of demonic influences or not.

What we must be mindful of is that in some cultures the enemy conceals himself, but just as surely does he shoot his arrows at us to hinder our journey to Christ. It may be a desire to fit in with friends, apathy towards our faith, doubt, fear, addiction, or something as seemingly mundane as laziness. Take a moment to ask which weapon would be most effective against you? Which would compromise committing more of your heart to Christ and leading a holier life? You can be sure that the enemy is working that angle. Be vigilant.

Alert and Praying,
Perseverance

WEEK SIX, DAY FIVE

"That they may set their hope in God,
And not forget the works of God,
But keep His commandments;
And may not be like their fathers,
A stubborn and rebellious generation,
A generation that did not set its heart aright,
And whose spirit was not faithful to God."
Psalm 78:7-8

Dear Brave Warrior,

I was on my lunch break at work, sitting at a big round table with my co-workers as we chatted about politics and complained about how things were heading. One older gentleman suddenly remarked, "Well, it doesn't matter to me. I'll be dead before that happens." I was stunned and a little hurt. Since he wouldn't be affected, he didn't care about the younger people who would have to deal with it. It wasn't his problem. How could he be so callous?

    I think some of the most frustrating and fiercest dragons come not from demons but from those who have walked the path before us. They walk along, oblivious to the things they've put in the way of those coming after them, uncaring about the consequences since they won't live to see them. I've been so disheartened by the seemingly insurmountable obstacles placed in my path by the generation ahead of me. But this isn't about me. This is about you, my dear friend coming up behind me on the journey. And my generation has plenty to answer for when it comes to ferocious dragons.

My young friend, I want to apologize to you. We on the path ahead of you have been tasked with your care. It is reasonable to expect us to be valiant warriors, slaying all before us, earnestly working to make your path at least a little safer than ours was, but we have failed. Instead, like the generations before us, we have looked only to ourselves. We have squandered your futures for our own immediate and temporary gratification. We are prideful, angry, greedy, and vindictive. We are full of violence and hate. We try to overly control you, blame you for our failures, criticize your concerns, and sometimes abandon you entirely. We have utterly turned away from the faith of our fathers. Some of the monsters you face, we loosed. Some of the walls in your way, we've built.

I have turned a blind eye from the things being done to our society, to our world, to you. I have, like this older gentleman, been too easy to dismiss a complaint that doesn't affect me personally. I have squandered wealth and resources. I have added to the burning division and hatred in our world, giving you a hostile, confusing, and depressing road to travel behind me. Please, if you can, forgive us- forgive me- for not being better than those that came before us, for making your path darker instead of lighter. If I could have one wish, it is for you to not follow in our mistakes. If I could have one prayer, it is that God would make you strong enough to slay our dragons and swift enough to jump our walls. In His mercy, I am confident that He will. May He also enable me to salvage what I can for you and be a helping hand instead of a devouring mouth. Go. Fight. Win.

A Sinner,
Steadfast

WEEK SIX, DAY SIX
LAZARUS SATURDAY

> *"Through God we will do valiantly,*
> *For it is He who shall tread down our enemies."*
> Psalm 60:12

Dear Proactive Helper,

Somehow, we expect that the antagonists of our pilgrimages will be obviously evil. In reality, we are drawn aside by seemingly benign forces: sports practices that are scheduled at the same time as evening services, the warmth of a bed on a cold Sunday morning, the ache to watch the latest episode of a favorite show when it will leave us too sleepy to pray. We try to pray, but a friend texts. We hear that there's a need for help at coffee hour, but we figure another person will volunteer. We see the classmate bullied every day, but we stay out of it. We retreat into our screens, into entertainment, when we feel overwhelmed, rather than persevering in hard tasks before us.

There was a time when I lived in Chile and was riding a bus home from my rowing club after training. Stepping off the bus at the terminal landed me in the middle of a fight. A man had just sliced at the head and neck of his uncle with a blade he yet brandished. A gathering crowd said nothing, did nothing but stare. Something changed in me, and I find it hard to articulate how it came to be, but God made me entirely fearless. I yelled at the man with the knife, ordering him back, and asking why he was doing this. I must have looked as fierce as I felt, for he dropped back. I focused on the bleeding man then, lowering him down to the ground in case he'd faint from shock. I wrapped my rowing pants around the worst wounds to staunch the bleeding, and spoke calmly to him, getting pertinent data. Then I focused on the crowd: CALL THE POLICE. CALL AN AMBULANCE. GET ME CLEAN WATER NOW. MOVE! NOW! The trance was broken and water was passed to me and phone calls were made. I kept an eye on the attacker, and was glad when the police arrived, followed by medics.

As they took the men away, there was nothing left to do but find somewhere to wash my bloody hands. I found a bathroom in the terminal, and as I scrubbed the crimson from my skin I began to shake uncontrollably. All of the borrowed strength was leaving, and I cried.

In the fight I had stumbled upon, the attacker was obviously doing evil, right? But there was also the passive evil of the crowd, the lethargic inaction, the mob mentality that thinks that surely someone else will do something. In our pilgrimage the lack of earnest focus can find us snoozing under a hedge, getting lost in a screen, or seeing something wrong but doing nothing, while fellow pilgrims need our help. Let us be on our guard against passive sins!

Fervently,
Perseverance

WEEK SIX, DAY SEVEN
PALM SUNDAY

"Blessed is the man
who walks not in the counsel of the wicked,
nor stands in the way of sinners,
nor sits in the seat of scoffers"
Psalm 1:1

Dear Precious Face in the Crowd,

Palm Sunday has always been a strange, bittersweet feast day for me. On the one hand, there is the jubilant procession of palms, the cry of "Hosanna in the Highest!" the excitement in the air as we have–at last!–arrived at Holy Week! And yet, this celebration rings hollow in my ears when I consider that Jesus entered Jerusalem knowing that He would be betrayed, tortured, and killed. There are many people in that palm-bearing crowd who will also be in the throng outside of Pontus Pilate's judgement seat. The lips shouting "Hosanna!" will later scream, "Crucify Him!" in only a matter of days.

Jesus knew all of this, even as He triumphantly entered the holy city. I wonder if He was able to look into that crowd and see exactly whose hearts of joy would soon turn to hate. It's a sobering thought: Why did this joyful crowd turn against their King? How could they go from rejoicing to condemning so quickly? Why kill their Messiah? Part of the answer is very simple: He failed to deliver what they expected.

The Jewish people in Jesus' time were under Roman occupation and rule. They were not a free nation, but they were ruled by foreigners and heathens. They longed for the day they could be released and see their enemies destroyed. When Jesus entered Jerusalem on that momentous Sunday, the crowds shouted because they thought their time had finally come: Jesus was entering Jerusalem at the opposite side of town from where the Roman proconsul was entering at the exact same time. Many of them thought that Jesus was a prophet about to reveal himself as a political leader coming to start a revolution! Surely the one who could perform such signs of power could overthrow a government. They made a parade because they thought that Jesus would overthrow Pilate and, eventually, the Roman Emperor. Their people would finally prosper again!

In their concern over their desire to rule themselves, they missed the fact that Jesus was here to rescue their souls, restore their community of lovingkindness with God at the heart of it, and free them from sin and death—powers much more destructive than the Romans! They were concerned with a particular vision of power in this world, not with God.

Our modern world is no different. People frequently leave the path of Christ for similar reasons: He fails to deliver what they think they want. Or they twist Jesus' words to focus on gain for their nation or race or political creed, missing the fact that the Son of God is Lord of *all* nations, races, and governments. They want Jesus to conform to their image, not the other way around. The hardest thing about these people is that they are many, and they are loud.

The mob mentality is pervasive in our culture, and Jesus rarely fits in with it. They are like tiny dragons who seem to be your friend, coming up to you as if they have your best intentions at heart, but then slowly nibbling away at your flesh until you can no longer stand. As long as you do what they want and adhere to their views, they laud you. But as soon as you point out a different path, you are demonized. It happened to Jesus, and He promises it will happen to His followers as well.

Be careful when the worldly dragons give you praise. It comes with a price: follow their wishes, or they will quickly crucify you, too. Walking this path through Holy Week is difficult and controversial, but man's praise is cheap when compared to the riches of eternity. Resist the mob, and follow the Master.

Standing With You,
Steadfast

WEEK SEVEN: FOLLOWING THE MASTER
TRACING CHRIST'S STEPS TO THE CROSS

WEEK SEVEN, DAY ONE
HOLY MONDAY

> *"The righteous shall flourish like a palm tree,*
> *He shall grow like a cedar in Lebanon.*
> *Those who are planted in the house of the Lord*
> *Shall flourish in the courts of our God."*
> Psalm 92:12-13

Dear Blossoming Virtue,

Our journey is nearly complete. Only one more week of fasting remains, and though the dragons are behind us, we must remain ever vigilant. We are now tracing the steps of Christ, putting our small feet within the divine footprints He's left behind on His way to the cross. He is so near to us now. With each passing day and within each service, we will hear His call echo louder and feel His touch as He takes our hand, guiding us ever forward through the Valley of the Shadow of Death. This might be the most terrifying part of our entire adventure, for there is no way to our Destination, to Pascha, to Christ, without going through this dark, damp, and lonely place. But take heart! As dark as it is, there is a Light, a Warmth, and a Presence with us. We do not walk alone.

Today begins our Bridegroom services. Last night, if you were at church, you would have heard the story of Jesus cursing the fig tree. You may have also heard songs about Joseph, whom the Church recognizes today as a prefiguration of Christ's Passion. Joseph had to endure betrayal, slavery, false accusations and a long imprisonment before he became one of the highest rulers of Egypt, rescuing his family and the entire region from famine in the process. This is Christ's journey as well, through the betrayal of Judas, the false accusations leveled at Him from the Pharisees, the torture of hanging on a cross, and the long three days in the bowels of Hades before Resurrection and Victory and Redemption for All. It is through here we must also go.

During these next few days, we will be admonished to check ourselves and the fruit we are bearing to ensure we are headed in the right direction and truly growing into Christlikeness. If our feet are on the correct path, it will show in how we live our lives, in the fruit we bear. The fig tree is a solemn reminder of that reality: if we are not allowing ourselves to be transformed, not giving room in our souls for Christ to abide within us, our branches will be barren. Then, when we finally come face to face with Jesus at the end of our lives, we will have proven ourselves false. But, there is still time! We are each still blossoming, working towards the season of fruit-bearing when our Lord will come to inspect His trees. He gives us everything we need to bear much fruit, including Himself! All we need to do is allow Him to work in us and run to Him in repentance when we fail to heed Him. He will always forgive. He will always aid us. We are never left to our own devices, for He longs to see and help us become fruitful trees.

This pilgrimage has been a preparation for that time, an exercise in growing fruit, a time to look at ourselves and ask honestly if Christ resides within us or if our growth is stunted. Sometimes it's going to feel like two steps forward and one step back. But take heart: our eternal Gardener loves each one of His trees and will always stoop to help the one who cries out to Him for mercy.

Rooted in Him,
Steadfast

WEEK SEVEN, DAY TWO
HOLY TUESDAY

> *"For exaltation comes neither from the east,*
> *Nor from the west, nor from the south.*
> *But God is the Judge:*
> *He puts down one,*
> *And exalts another."*
> Psalm 75:6-7

Dear Daughter, not Granddaughter, of God,

I had gone to venerate a myrrh-streaming icon at a local parish. The nave was packed with people, and I needed to leave halfway through the service to nurse my baby. When I tried to re-enter the church, ushers blocked me from going in, because people were starting to go forward to venerate, and they didn't want anyone from the narthex cutting in line. My baby squirmed in my arms, and I looked sadly at the clock; my husband would need me home soon, and because I'd lost my place, there was no way I could now wait for hundreds to go before me.

Just then some young ladies breezed into the narthex, having just arrived. One moaned to the other that it would take too long to go forward, and the other laughed, saying that it would be fine, because her relatives were priests, and they'd let them go right in. Sure enough, the women strode right past the ushers and right up to the icon. Encouraged slightly that maybe they'd let me in too, since otherwise I'd have no opportunity, I asked the ushers if I too might pass, because I could not stay longer. The answer was a resolute, "no." Tears streaming, I dashed to my car, denied access to a miracle because I wasn't "in." I wasn't a priest's granddaughter or niece; I was just a flustered, unknown mom with a fussy baby.

Men make errors that God never makes. God is interested in His children, not on whom they are connected to, however illustrious and good. You will not get to the day of judgment and be asked how faithful your parents were. You cannot borrow holiness.

Today we remember the parable of the wise and foolish virgins. Ten went out to meet the bridegroom, five wise ones with oil in their lamps, and five foolish ones without oil. They all fell asleep waiting for him, symbolizing death that awaits all. When the bridegroom appeared at midnight, they all rose up to go to him, and the foolish ones realized that they didn't have oil to light the way. They asked the wise ones for some, but the wise ones knew they'd need all their oil, and told them to go and purchase their own. While they were gone, the bridegroom arrived, and they went into the wedding. The foolish ones arrived late, only to find the door shut, and they asked to be let in. The Lord answered, "Assuredly, I say to you, I do not know you."

The wise virgins weren't selfish, but rather represent how impossible it is to borrow righteousness and preparedness from another in the final judgment; it is something that each must attend to personally beforehand. Is there oil in your lamp? It won't matter if your parents have oil, nor your grandparents, nor your godparents. You must be ready, for, "Behold, the Bridegroom comes at midnight, and blessed is the servant whom He shall find watching."

Checking The Oil,
Perseverance

WEEK SEVEN, DAY THREE
HOLY WEDNESDAY

> *"All who hate me whisper together against me;*
> *Against me they devise my hurt.*
> *"An evil disease," they say, "clings to him.*
> *And now that he lies down, he will rise up no more."*
> *Even my own familiar friend in whom I trusted,*
> *Who ate my bread,*
> *Has lifted up his heel against me."*
> Psalm 41: 7-9

Dear Broken Heart,

Today Judas has met with the Pharisees and made a plan to betray his Lord and Best Friend. It is a grim day. Pure love has been stabbed in the back for a bit of gain, a fleeting handful of silver. It's outrageous. Unfortunately, it is not rare.

Have you been betrayed? I have. It cuts deep. The shock gives way to rage which burns out into grief then turns to attack your very being: how could I have let this happen? Why am I so stupid? I must have deserved it. Sometimes a betrayal comes at the hand of a friend who feigns love but spreads lies behind our backs. Sometimes it takes the form of a family member who uses our trust to hurt us, sometimes in unspeakable and intimate ways. Sometimes a person of power like a teacher or a church leader uses their position to maim us, destroying our confidence and sometimes even our bodies and souls. When this happens, our faith quivers and threatens to fall. We have done nothing but love and trust these people, and in return we have received only brokenness and pain.

Jesus felt this same shattering. Tomorrow night He will look out over His last meal with His friends and know that someone He loves has traded His life for money. We scoff at how Judas could betray the Son of God, but all around us these same betrayals happen, as lives are destroyed all so that someone else can receive a few moments of pleasure or a few extra dollar bills. It's easy to do. It's hard to recover from.

Today, give your pain to God. Know that He personally understands betrayal and does not tolerate it. You did not deserve it. You aren't stupid. If you've been betrayed by a seemingly religious person, don't let that shape your view of God, for He does not trick us nor stab us in the back nor use His power to abuse us. These things are of Satan. Renounce them and resolve to never sell someone's trust for your own gain. Learn from this moment, and let it shape you further into the image of Christ.

Perhaps it is apt that many churches administer the sacrament of Holy Unction on this day. After all that we have walked through, fought, and endured, betrayal can feel like the last straw, the knife in the back that threatens to do us in. We are heartsick and desperately need divine help. If your parish offers it, try not miss this holy service, this healing touch of God. Let it seep into your broken body and soul as a balm. Mix your tears with those of Christ's in the Gethsemane and take comfort that ours is a God who feels and knows pain. Better yet: He turns it to good and smothers it in love and victory. May He embrace you tightly.

Yours in Faith,
Steadfast

WEEK SEVEN, DAY FOUR
HOLY THURSDAY

"My God, My God, why have You forsaken Me?
Why are you so far from helping Me,
And from the words of My groaning?"
Psalm 22:1

Dear Humbled One,

We were spiritually homeless for a while, having left our faith tradition on the road to becoming Orthodox. This worried our family, particularly my husband's great aunt. She was in her mid-eighties, and though spry, she seemed increasingly frail each year. She arrived at our home for a visit, a basin and towel tucked under her arm. "I've come to wash your feet," she declared in her no-nonsense way, and there was no telling her otherwise.

Seeing a wonderfully holy elderly woman get down on her knees on our hard wooden floors was almost more than I could bear. She lovingly washed each of our feet, tenderly drying between each toe. She was so concerned that we weren't settled in a home church, so she brought church into our home. It was one of the most humbling and holy moments of my life.

Today we remember several pivotal moments of Holy Week, including Christ washing His disciples' feet. They, too, felt altogether unworthy; that the Highest should do the work of the lowest, the slaves, was unfathomable. He showed His disciples once again what He meant by saying, "Whoever desires to become great among you shall be your servant."

After washing their feet, our Lord broke bread, blessed it, and gave it to His disciples saying, "Take, eat; this is My body." Then He took wine, gave thanks, and gave it to them saying, "Drink from it, all of you. For this is My blood of the new covenant, which is shed for many for the remission of sins." Did you ever notice that Judas, too, was served the Eucharist? God in His infinite love desires each of His children to repent, to return to Him, no matter what they have done or become.

In the dark of night, they walked to the Garden of Gethsemane. Our Lord was in agony, knowing all that was to come. He said to His disciples, "My soul is exceedingly sorrowful, even to death. Stay here and watch with Me." The disciples fell asleep. Three times He asked them to watch and pray with Him, and three times they dozed off. Our Lord suffered alone in the dark garden, praying and weeping.

Then, Judas came. "Friend, why have you come?" With a kiss the betrayal was complete, and the chief priests and elders arrested Him. They came to snuff out the Light of the world, the Giver of Life, the Messiah, the King of All. The One who humbly washes feet, who offers Himself eternally in bread and wine, who willingly passes through agony in order to free us from the power of sin and death.

Trying To Watch and Pray,
Perseverance

WEEK SEVEN, DAY FIVE
GREAT AND HOLY FRIDAY

"The sorrows of Sheol surrounded me;
The snares of death confronted me.
In my distress I called upon the Lord
And cried out to my God;"
Psalm 18:5-6

Dear Immortal Soul,

The shadow of the cross has fallen upon us. Christ is broken and bleeding, torturously living out His last moments, His breath finally leaving His body. His mother wails, His disciples gape in shock, and we are left to gaze at the reminder of our mortality; we are here in the Valley of the Shadow of Death.

I was a middle schooler when the Columbine school shooting made national headlines. It was a shocking, monstrous event that left everyone asking, "How could this happen?" It seemed like something out of a horror story. Now, we have added Virginia Tech, Sandy Hook, Parkland, and a myriad of other school names to our list, each written in the blood of youth. By the time I was in high school, death was on my mind every day. I imagined what I would do if a shooter entered my school. I walked in each morning wondering if it would be my last. Some days, I still find myself watching doors, planning exits and escapes, just in case.

People used to comment that you feel invincible when you're young, that death feels so far away. I doubt whether that's still true. Death is breathing down the necks of young and old alike. I lost a fifteen-year-old cousin in a freak car accident that happened just outside his school. I've had close family members nearly die of drug overdose or eating disorders. The 2020 pandemic brought death into every sphere of life. And, of course, there is the silent killer of the young: suicide.

I'm willing to bet that death is not far from your thoughts, though you may, like most of the world, try to push it away, distracting yourself from it, or desperately try to do as much as you can in case you meet it early. Perhaps you know someone who has died. Perhaps, today, you are grieving.

Death is inevitable. It is the only certainty in life. No matter who you are or what you do, you will die. Does that scare you? Do you let that reality seep into you, or do you resist and try to push it away as fast as you can, ignoring it?

Does it give you anxiety to think of it? St. Hesychios wrote in the *Philokalia* (a collection of beautiful and good sayings of early church teachers) that we must always be watching our thoughts, trying to draw them away from the passions (misdirected or confused strengths) and settling them on Christ instead. One way to do this, he taught, was to keep in mind your own death. Don't let yourself be distracted from it, but don't let fear engulf you. We should be able to look at death as a fact, a door that we must all pass through. Tonight, when we enter the church under the Altar, we enter Christ's own death. We are not alone even in the tomb. We all share in His death and will share in His Resurrection.

When you face death with Christ tonight, ask Him to shape your life. Our world pressures you to have many priorities in this life, but which ones matter in light of eternity? Ask the women who wept at the foot of the Cross to help you face life in the shadow of death. Today, tears are most welcome. But, do not forget one very important thing about death: it does not have the last word.

Holding You Close,
Steadfast

WEEK SEVEN, DAY SIX
HOLY SATURDAY

"But I have trusted in Your mercy;
My heart shall rejoice in Your salvation."
Psalm 13:5

Dear On the Cusp,

This day is stretched tight between the great sorrow of Holy Friday and the bright joy of Pascha, the tension palpable, the very air is charged with anticipation. The disciples are in mourning, hiding in fear; their hopes crushed and hearts broken. The tomb is sealed with cold finality. The Theotokos is awakening on the first day without her beloved Son.

In church this morning, the light is already pushing back the dark. We sing, "Arise, O God, judge thou the earth; for thou shall inherit among all the nations," as the priest throws bay leaves or flowers. We remember Christ descending into Hades, stripping it of its power, and destroying death. We make a joyous clamor of noise to celebrate the crashing down of the doors, the crushing of the chains, and smashing of the locks. Jesus's body yet lays motionless in the tomb, but He is also busting up Hades!

We carry that light home with us, beginning preparations for tonight's service, even if that just means everyone taking naps. For me the tsoureki bread is rising, rich with butter, milk, and eggs. My husband is marinating meat, and every smell is a torture and a delight. A large basket is lined with clean linen and piles of candles and wax-catching cups sit ready. Onion skins boil on the stove for dyeing eggs. There seems to be too much time and also not enough. The Bridegroom cometh!

In the dark we solemnly file into the nave. It is a quiet that has a smile to it. Behind the altar a flicker of light pierces the darkness and we hear, "Come receive the light from the Light that was never overtaken by night, and glorify Christ who is risen from the dead." We stream forward, each bending our candle into the flame, and bearing our light, the church growing brighter and brighter. The darkness retreats, and our songs remind it that it is a beaten foe.

We are almost there, dear one. The priest pounds on the doors and calls out, "Lift up your gates, ye princes, and be ye lifted up, ye everlasting doors; and the King of Glory shall come in." A reader within shouts, "Who is this King of Glory?" The priest shouts, "The Lord strong and mighty. The Lord mighty in battle. THE LORD OF THE POWERS. HE IS THE KING OF GLORY."

Breath Caught,
Perseverance

WEEK SEVEN, DAY SEVEN
GREAT AND GLORIOUS PASCHA

"Our God is the God of salvation;
And to God the Lord belong escapes from death."
Psalm 68:20

Dear Breathless,

Into quiet, into stillness, into dark cave's black
A sharp intake of breath
Linen wrappings stretch upward, filling
Eyes that death had closed now open
Light of the world un-snuffed
God arises

Gloating demons uncross their arms
Now unsmiling
Eyes widening
Lips curling, throats screaming
No! And then silence
Dry, black ash their only trace

Truest Life now sitting
Unswaddling, tingling limbs refilling
Blood coursing
He stretches
And looks to the mess
As Mom would, folding

The rock with gritty friction moving
Light in crescent arc widening
Walks the risen LORD, RISEN FROM THE DEAD

Trampling Down Death,
Perseverance and Steadfast

WEEK EIGHT: INTO THE KINGDOM
BASKING IN HIS LIGHT

WEEK EIGHT, DAY ONE
BRIGHT MONDAY

"Praise Him with the sound of the trumpet;
Praise Him with the lute and harp!
Praise Him with the timbrel and dance;
Praise Him with stringed instruments and flutes!
Praise Him with loud cymbals;
Praise Him with clashing cymbals!
Let everything that has breath praise the Lord.
Praise the Lord!"
Psalm 150:3-6

Dear Jubilant Dancer,

Christ is Risen!

Just because we have finished our Lenten journey doesn't mean that we will abandon you here in this new place. Allow us to show you around and celebrate with you just a bit longer! You are probably a bit overwhelmed. So many foods to try, so much more time on your hands! A lot has just happened, and yet our world spins on, almost oblivious to the incredible miracle that has taken place. There is still school to attend, jobs to work, responsibilities to fulfill. All has changed, and yet nothing has changed. It is a dizzying feeling.

Don't let the humdrum of the outside world affect your inner joy. Christ is Risen! Let this great truth sing in your heart! The long pilgrimage of tears and struggles has ended, and Christ is victorious. This is cause for celebration! Does it seem to you as if the world has forgotten how to celebrate? It's as though we teeter between two extremes: work without pause or play without meaning.

I've known people who turn their noses up at any idea of celebration, viewing it as frivolous, distrusting any strong happiness as fleeting or even sinful. On the other hand, I've known people who do nothing but seek pleasure and reasons to party, to the point where the celebrations become ends in themselves. They have no goal, no purpose, and eventually cause harm to the soul.

Solomon writes in Ecclesiastes, "To everything there is a season, a time for every purpose under heaven," including, "a time to mourn, and a time to dance." We are to be neither constant stoics nor reckless partiers. There is nothing wrong with celebration; indeed, God prescribed feasts and celebrations as part of the Law He gave to His people Israel. It's not just that we are allowed to celebrate, but we should! And yet those celebrations must be rooted in Christ. After all, what better reason do we have to celebrate?

Christ is victorious! He has given us everything! We are free! We are alive! We are healed! Celebrate, my friend! Dance! Sing! Laugh! Let the world mock us if they want, who cares? Christ is Risen! Indeed, He is Risen! If they knew what we knew, they'd be dancing too. All the angels in heaven are rejoicing. Let us shout along with them.

Twirling and Laughing,
Steadfast

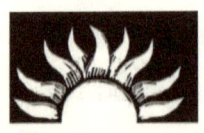

WEEK EIGHT, DAY TWO
BRIGHT TUESDAY

The Lord is my light and my salvation;
Whom shall I fear?
Psalm 27:1

Dear Full of Cheese,

Christ is Risen!

When Moses was told by God to build the tabernacle in the wilderness, the people donated their gold, wood, fiber, and skills, and within a short time they had a beautiful and portable temple in which to offer their sacrifices and worship God. Before all the people, God sent fire to consume the offering on the altar, and that fire was kept burning; even when they broke camp to follow God's leading cloud pillar, they brought the coals with them, using them to light the next fire. This was a tangible reminder of God's power and presence with them.

In Jerusalem, the Holy Fire is being passed from person to person, church to church, boarding planes and trains and buses, after descending upon Christ's tomb in the Church of the Holy Sepulchre on Saturday. This yearly miracle even reaches those of us on the other side of the world, as the flame is flown over the oceans in lanterns to share with the faithful. It came one year to our own parish, and I got to experience the warmth and wonder of it. From God, to a bundle of candles in the hands of a Patriarch all the way to our little parish in Pennsylvania, to a candle in my own shaking hands. Wow.

Let us think about fire for a moment: it gives light, it gives warmth, it consumes, and it spreads. I can think of no metaphor more apt for the work of the Holy Spirit on our hearts. He illumines, He warms us with love, and we overflow, spreading that light, that fire, to others. That is...if we let it spread.

We can make a simple though tragic error here. We can receive and not give. Horribly, we can even think that we're the only ones meant to have the fire, because we are Greek or Russian or Eritrean. Perhaps we think it's nicer to keep our faith discreet, filing it under "My Culture" or "My Heritage," rather than remembering that Christ came to save, to reach the lost, and that He calls us to be a part of spreading the good news to all, regardless of ethnicity. When we do, we will become like those that St. John Chrysostom described when he said, "If but ten among us lead a holy life, we shall kindle a fire which shall light up an entire city." The fire is meant to keep going, to light up the whole world.

What will you do with the good news of Christ's resurrection? What will you do with your Paschal joy? Is it for you only to enjoy? Dare you risk spreading the fire?

With Work To Do,
Perseverance

WEEK EIGHT, DAY THREE
BRIGHT WEDNESDAY

"Oh, give thanks to the Lord, for He is good!
For His mercy endures forever.
Let the redeemed of the Lord say so,
Whom He has redeemed from the hand of the enemy,
And gathered out of the lands,
From the east and from the west,
From the north and from the south.

They wandered in the wilderness in a desolate way;
They found no city to dwell in.
Hungry and thirsty,
Their soul fainted in them.

Then they cried out to the Lord in their trouble,
And He delivered them out of their distresses.
And He led them forth by the right way,
That they might go to a city for a dwelling place.

Oh, that men would give thanks to the Lord for His goodness,
And for His wonderful works to the children of men!

> *For He satisfies the longing soul,*
> *And fills the hungry soul with goodness."*
> Psalm 107:1-9

Dear Story-Bearer,

Christ is Risen!

Come back to the desert, where St. Mary of Egypt has recounted her story to an amazed St. Zosimas. She bids him to pray for her, and to return on Holy Thursday of the next year and meet her at the Jordan River with the Holy Mysteries with him, telling no one of her life until she had reposed. When Abba Zosimas returned at the appointed time, she appeared at the other side of the Jordan. He wondered how she'd cross without a boat, but she made the sign of the cross over the water, and then walked upon it.

After receiving the Holy Mysteries, she asked him to return the next year to the place they'd first spoken, and again she walked over the Jordan River as before. Abba Zosimas kept her story in his heart, telling no one, regretting that he'd forgotten to ask her name.

When a year had passed, he returned to the place and found her body. Beside her she had written in the sand:

Abba Zosimas, bury on this spot the body of humble Mary. Return to dust what is dust. Pray to the Lord for me. I reposed on the first day of April, on the very night of the saving Passion of Christ, after partaking of the Mystical Supper.

In sorrow he looked about for some means of burying her, but the ground was hard, dry, and unyielding. Looking up, he saw a tremendous lion standing by her, licking her feet. Startled, Zosimas crossed himself and asked the lion to dig the grave. The lion obeyed, providing a final place of rest for our beloved Mary. Can you even imagine the honor of it? The king of the beasts digging a grave?

Abba Zosimas carried her story out of the desert with him. His fellow monks were astonished by her story, and to the present day her life of radical repentance continues to challenge and inspire us. Zosimas bore witness to the work of God in the heart of one woman. His story-bearing became a gift to generations of Christians to draw strength from.

In the same way, these letters bear witness to the patient and persistent work of God in our lives. We are no perfect women, but even so we see how the darkness has receded, how the light has seeped into our hearts, and how the broken bits are being made whole. We see how God was protecting, guiding, teaching, disciplining, and comforting us as we journeyed toward Him. That two once-Protestant Christians, a Goth and a Tree-Hugger would be guided by Him to the same path, walking side by side into His Holy Church is astonishing. That He had story-bearing work to do together is even more so.

You too bear witness, dear fellow pilgrim. Your story matters, not just for yourself, but for others as well. You carry a story unique in time, your own, and no one else can tell it. It can become water for the thirsty, comfort for the grieved, inspiration for the broken. Journey well, dear friend.

With All My Love,
Perseverance

WEEK EIGHT, DAY FOUR
BRIGHT THURSDAY

"Trust in Him at all times, you people;
Pour out your heart before Him;
God is a refuge for us."
Psalm 62:8

Dear Among the Knots,

Christ is Risen!

There's so much that we do not see in the moment, dear one. I am old enough now to look back at all the twists and turns of my life, and bear witness to God's constant kindness to me. I am young enough still that I remember that in the moments themselves I thought my life was ending, cursed, or ruined. The boy I had a heartsick crush on wasn't interested in me. I failed an important test. I couldn't afford to go to university and imagined my life would be dull gray, passed under fluorescent lights in a factory somewhere. I could not see what He was doing, what He was teaching me, what He was preparing me for, and that it was good.

We have a tendency to judge the events of our lives wrongly, or at least, prematurely, when faith shows us beauties, goodness, and truth that comes through ways that are often counter-intuitive. By not being able to go to university, I met my wonderful husband, and after twenty years we even still like each other! When we painfully separated from our faith tradition due to theological issues, we were unknowingly on the road to the Orthodox Church! Some of the best things that ever happened to me did not look good nor pleasant at the time. They were hard, they hurt.

If you've ever seen a piece of embroidered cloth, you'll know that the front has a gorgeous, intricate design, but that the back is all knots, wild thread tails, and chaos. We live among the knots in the present. We don't know exactly what God is going to make of this mess. We can't see the beauty, the design...yet.

Trusting,
Perseverance

WEEK EIGHT, DAY FIVE
BRIGHT FRIDAY

"By You I have been upheld from birth;
You are He who took me out of my mother's womb.
My praise shall be continually of You.."
Psalm 71:6

Dear Made In His Image,

Christ is Risen!

Can you imagine what it must have been like to head toward a grave that early Sunday morning, Passover Sabbath ended, tears still fresh on your cheeks as you clutch your precious ointments and cloths to properly bury One who changed your life? You worry about many things: Were the guards cruel to His body? Is He already decomposing? Will we be in trouble if we're caught? How will we ever convince them to roll away that monstrous stone? But you arrive, and the guards are passed out in a heap. The stone is casually rolled off to the side, and His body is gone. You're immediately frightened and outraged. Who would have dared desecrate His grave like this?! Are the thieves nearby? Will they hurt me?

But then, He's there, shining, glorious, standing before you and more beautiful than you've ever seen Him before. The warmth of His face spreads through you, deep into your very center, filling you in places you never knew were empty. Your soul alights, jumping in joy as if it cannot be contained by flesh any longer. You feel as though, if He only touched you, you could fly straight to the heavens. He says your name. He asks you to tell His disciples. You shake all over, adrenaline coursing through your veins as you run back to the city, one thought playing over and over in your head: He is alive! I have seen the Lord!

Why did Jesus appear to His women disciples, the holy myrrh-bearers coming to anoint His dead body? Women were not highly viewed in ancient Jewish society. They were property, unable to even be counted as witnesses in court because, "a woman's testimony wasn't to be trusted." But they, like the male disciples, had followed Jesus throughout His ministry. They had cared for Him out of their own resources, even gathering the burial spices that they were bringing that morning. They knew that they were His, not as His property, but as His creatures and students. They saw in Him the One who made them. He looked at the women disciples, the cast-offs of powerful society, and valued them.

If this were a man-made fairytale, Jesus would have appeared to His more reputable male disciples first, or maybe Pontus Pilate, or perhaps the Pharisees, scaring them as He gloriously shouted, "I told you so!" But, no, Jesus chose to appear first to women of little consequence, thereby making them important and erasing their shame. Women were the first to behold His resurrected body. Women matter to God.

Throughout His life, Jesus had cared for women, whether in His love for Mary and Martha as He wept with them and brought their brother back to life, the healing of Mary Magdalene from seven demons, the forgiving of the woman caught in adultery, or His precious Mother whom He cherished, obeyed, and made sure would be taken care of after His death. God made both man and woman in His image. There are subtle (and even not-so-subtle) messages out there telling you that you are worth less than a man, that you have little value in heaven. These messages are not of God, but of human pride. Guard your heart from them.

Christ is Risen, and He chose to tell women first, thereby affirming our value. We may be different with unique roles to play, but our worth before God is neither less nor more than any man's. Hold that truth in your heart as a flame, letting it warm you against the cold of social bigotry.

Full of Love,
Steadfast

WEEK EIGHT, DAY SIX
BRIGHT SATURDAY

"Be still, and know that I am God"
Psalm 46:10

Dear Fully Present,

Christ is Risen!

On a walk on a local trail, I veered off into the woods, following a gurgling stream to a secluded spot, overhung by dense branches. I stilled my body, and I became small, my arms enfolding my legs as I sat by the water. The birds and minnows soon forgave and forgot my intrusion, and I became part of the landscape, so to speak. I heard the tones the birds used to speak with one another, I marveled at the small worlds found in dew drops nestled in the leaves. I noticed my breathing and the sounds of the water, and the textures of the bark and stones. I was fully where I was.

My dear one, sometimes you'll just have to silence the ever-jabbering, ever-buzzing, ever-dinging phone, for it is likely tethered to your heart. Like moths we're drawn to the light, away from where we are, where our bodies are. Snip the tether; the world within it can wait. Be where your body is, fully there. Notice the impulse to check the phone, how your hand will hover over the pocket you keep it in. Ask yourself why, and investigate that impulse. Why is it so hard to just be where you are?

We had arrived in Dublin for an epic road trip around the green isle. After procuring our rental car, we attempted to safely drive on the left side of the road, seated on the right side of the car, shifting gears left-handedly, through unfamiliar roads with dubious signage. We poured over the road map, trying to navigate with some order out of the urban jungle. There were so many distractions, that we hardly even saw the ancient, beautiful city that we were driving through. Our eyes darted from map to stick shift to road sign to map, and so on. Once we got out of the city, however, the Irish countryside completely engulfed our senses. We pulled over to explore the ruins of a stronghold in a field. No longer were our eyes darting about busily, but we were instead noticing: the smell of the flowers, the lichen on the stone walls, the steady creep of rain clouds over the fields, and the "baaaaaaa!" of herds of sheep. We were present in the present.

I am old enough to know the difference between the times before smartphones and after them. I've seen how we've become chronically "away" from each other, staring into screens. Families sit at restaurant tables, not speaking to each other, everyone privately entertained, scrolling. I meet a friend for coffee, but half the time she is texting, scrolling, checking...away. Children who used to interact with others at the grocery stores now sit hunched over a device.

The way before us requires attention, presence, and stillness. Dear one, be not always away.

Ye Olde Dinosaur,
Perseverance

WEEK EIGHT, DAY SEVEN
THOMAS SUNDAY

*"The Lord who made heaven and earth
Bless you from Zion!"*
Psalm 134:3

Dear Horizon-Bound,

Christ is Risen!

We have come, at last, to the true end of our journey together. We have traveled far and wide, conquered many an obstacle and slain many a beast. We have resolved to seek Christ and abide in Him, following in His steps, even through the grave, that we may also follow in His glorious Resurrection. We have embraced healing and freedom, celebrating the immeasurable love and power found within our great God. But, wait! It looks like one person is late to the party!

Today the Church recognizes St. Thomas, the last (but certainly not least) of the Disciples to see the Resurrected Christ. Can you imagine poor Thomas' frustration, to have been out and about and miss seeing Jesus when He appeared to everyone else in the upper room? I often wonder if the words of doubt that we now associate with him weren't more an outburst of disappointment. All of his friends had witnessed the Supreme Miracle...and he had just barely missed it. How upsetting!

This journey of ours through Lent is a smaller version of our journey through life. What we do during Lent helps us to focus on the larger context of our lives, to home in and re-examine who we are and who Christ is. It is my hope and prayer that you have grown more in Christ-likeness, that this season has been beneficial for you.

But, sometimes, we just barely miss Him. Something else has grabbed our attention and called us away, and while others have come through Lent having encountered God, we are late to the party. Was this Lent harder than normal? Do you feel as though your journey bore little fruit? Are you not able to celebrate, spirit too exhausted or disappointed? Take heart! Thomas was late, but Jesus did not abandon him. He appeared once again and let St. Thomas touch Him. He gave Thomas such an encounter, that he could only exclaim, "My Lord and my God!" while he worshipped Him.

As with Lent, our life sometimes feels like two steps forward and one step back. We will be frustrated, disappointed, and often feel as if we are losing our way. But keep trudging forward. Jesus is coming. He will not abandon you! Even if you are "late," there is an encounter with Christ waiting for you.

St. Thomas would go on from his encounter to evangelize India. To this day, Christians there trace their spiritual heritage back to this once-tardy saint. So, you see, it is not the timing that matters, it is Christ. Whether you experienced Him this Lent or not, He is with you, and He will empower you for the journey ahead.

We hope these letters and lessons stay close to your heart. Feel free to revisit them any time you need! May what we've experienced together this Lent never leave us, but continue to shape us as we go ever forward on our pilgrimage toward holiness, victory, and God in the Flesh. We look forward to the day we can embrace you in person at journey's end in the presence of our Resurrected King. Christ is Risen, dear one! Truly, He is Risen!

Until That Glorious Day,
Steadfast and Perseverance

REFERENCES

WEEK ONE, DAY THREE: St. Mark the Ascetic, *Homilies*, 1.54

WEEK TWO, DAY SIX: *Dorotheos of Gaza: Discourses and Sayings*, p. 247-248, Cistercian Publication, (St. Gennadius of Constantinople, *The Golden Chain*, 53-55)

WEEK THREE, DAY SIX: St. Basil the Great, from *Homily V. In martyrem Julittam* This modern translation excerpt is found at http://www.orthodoxchurchquotes.com/2014/11/27/st-basil-the-great-when-you-sit-down-to-eat/

WEEK FOUR, DAY ONE: St. John Chrysostom's *Homilies on the Statutes*

WEEK FOUR, DAY THREE: (St. Silouan the Athonite, *Writings*, IX.27)

WEEK SEVEN, DAY TWO: Matthew 25:12, Holy Tuesday troparion

WEEK SEVEN, DAY FOUR: Mark 10:43, Matthew 26:26, Matthew 26:27,28, Matthew 26:50

WEEK EIGHT, DAY TWO: St. John Chrysostom, "On Living Simply"

ABOUT THE AUTHORS

Sarah Gingrich is a writer, blogger, poet, and contributing author in *Darkness Is As Light* (Park End Books, 2020). When not writing, she runs a small soapmaking company, keeps bees, gardens, and mothers her brood of six children with her forbearing husband.

Brought up as an evangelical Protestant in Montana, Sarah lived out her faith and worked many years overseas as a missionary, gathering stories as she transitioned from country to country and was led from her evangelical Protestant faith into Orthodoxy. Now Pennsylvania-based, she enjoys hiking, kayaking, and observing the natural world around her.

To read more of her journey, visit thelivescript.com.

A. N. Tallent is a writer, reader, gamer, and full-time mom. She lives in southern Pennsylvania but has also called Florida and Illinois home.

Tallent studied Missions at an evangelical Bible college and went on many short-term mission trips to the country of Japan. She also worked for five years at a large evangelical missions organization, where she grew in her love for various cultures and the broad perspective of the world that inspires her writing.

Her adventures led her to join the Eastern Orthodox Church in 2018, where she has found peace and a deeper understanding of Christ.

She made her publication debut as a contributing author to *Darkness Is As Light* (Park End Books, 2020). She identifies as a gothic Christian and an Adult Survivor of Child Abuse, which is reflected in her unique voice and desire to use her words to reach out to the hurting.

ABOUT PARK END BOOKS

Park End Books is a traditional small press bringing to market accessible curricula and emerging Catholic, Orthodox, and other creedal Christian authors. Visit us online at ParkEndBooks.com.

COMING SOON FROM PARK END BOOKS

Apocalypse: Managed

by Jonathan Andrew

(May 2021)

This humorous fantasy novel follows a close-knit group of friends and control freaks through the last day of Earth. Deeply insightful and laugh out loud funny, Jonathan Andrew's book is reminiscent of the styles of both C.S. Lewis and Douglas Adams.

Into the Flames & Other Plays on Saints' Lives

by Christine Siampos

(May 2021)

These six accessible plays by playwright and Orthodox priest's daughter Christine Siampos help to anchor youth groups in the stories of the saints. Into the Flames is part of the Park End Books Accessible Church School curriculum line.

Our Autistic Home

by Summer Kinard

(Autumn 2021)

Learn how to make your household into a place where autistic family members thrive. Kinard brings the wisdom garnered from life in an all-autistic household to help families plan, adapt, understand, and remove handicaps to autistic functioning so that everyone feels truly at home. With the easy to apply tips and resources in this book, you can start a new era of joy for your entire family.

www.ingramcontent.com/pod-product-compliance
Lightning Source LLC
Chambersburg PA
CBHW021441070526
44577CB00002B/247